What Makes Bend Special

WHAT MAKES
BEND
SPECIAL...

Discovering
Your Place in the
Pacific Northwest's
Most Dynamic
Community

JIM SCHELL

For distribution information please call:
Lights On Publishing
541 788-7137
Bend, Oregon

Printed in the United States of America

ABOUT THE AUTHOR

Jim Schell is an old guy who refuses to retire. Instead, he spends his waking hours looking for ways to help his community become a better place to live. He's learned that for a community to thrive, it needs jobs, schools, recreation opportunities, and most of all, the right kind of people. This book is for, and about, those people.

Before moving to Bend in 1994, Jim started four successful Minneapolis companies over a 25-year entrepreneurial career. Since moving here, he has started six nonprofits (including Opportunity Knocks, the managing partner of this book), fixed four broken ones, and written a dozen or so business books (mostly for the sheer pleasure of sharing his experiences with those folks who want to learn from his mistakes). He's also watched his golf game deteriorate faster'n a deer can devour a flower garden. He mentors dozens of Bend's future leaders and is one lucky guy to be the husband of Mary, father to Jim, Todd and Mike, and a card-carrying citizen of Bend, the most energetic, slam-dandiest town this side of the Statue of Liberty.

MORE ABOUT THE AUTHOR

What makes Bend special? One key ingredient comes in the form of Jim Schell—a man who can't and won't toot his own horn, but that horn must be tooted. He is a connector, a fire starter, a mentor, and a magic maker. His energy is endless, and he's an entrepreneur in business and in life. He knows how to take an idea and add the right people with the right resources to make things happen.

Jim holds the bar high and makes us want to jump for it. He's not afraid to get his hands dirty, and he's not afraid to have the tough conversations. He can make you feel like a thousand bucks, or he can bring you to tears, because you know he cares, all the while taking no spoils for himself. His payment is the satisfaction that comes from helping others. His selfless acts have changed Bend and continue to do so. Not every community has a Jim Schell. He's one of a kind.

Julie Miller, —Retired, First Interstate Banker EVP

Jim Schell's passion for helping Bend's entrepreneurs, small-business owners, and nonprofits translates into Bend's vibrant economic ecosystem. His guidance, drive, and get-sh*t-done attitude leaves a lasting legacy of successful organizations in his wake. One of Jim's fascinating traits is his desire to be constantly learning; he's continually reinventing himself and pushing the edge of his abilities. Jim has upgraded to version 9.0 and is currently working on 10.0 status. I am honored to have him as my friend and mentor.

Preston Callicott, —CEO, Five Talent Software

THANKS TO...

Organizing Partner

Opportunity Knocks (OK): OK assembles and facilitates advisory-board teams of business owners and entrepreneurs, with the purpose of helping each other solve problems and achieve success. Started in 1996, OK's concept of peers helping peers through the use of volunteer facilitators has stood the test of time. Hundreds of Bend businesses have enjoyed OK's collaborative approach to problem solving. *opp-knocks.org*.

Funding and Distribution Partners

Bend Chamber of Commerce: Bend's Chamber of Commerce includes 1,200 members from its business community. The Chamber mobilizes its members to help them succeed while at the same time serving as an advocate for business. The Chamber's unique programs include the education and training of young leaders (Leadership Bend) and a robust intern program for college and high school students. *bendchamber.org*.

Brooks Resources: Black Butte Ranch, Northwest Crossing, North Rim, Awbrey Glen, Awbrey Butte, Mt. Bachelor Village Resort, Ironhorse—sound familiar? They're all Brooks Resources developments. As one of Bend's foremost and finest corporate citizens, Brooks Resources has been in business for nearly 50 years. *brooksresources.com*.

Cascade Relays Foundation: The Cascade Lakes Relay is a 216-mile, overnight, team event. It is a race, a celebration, and a vacation all wrapped into one. The biggest winners are the nonprofits that benefit from the dollars that are raised by the Foundation; since 2008 that number is $300,000. *cascaderelays.com.*

Central Oregon Association of Realtors (COAR): 1,900 members strong, COAR is the voice of the real estate industry and the largest service provider in the region. In addition to offering a wide variety of educational services to its members, COAR is also the owner of Central Oregon's MLS system. *coar.com.*

Deschutes Brewery: In a town known for its active beer scene, Deschutes Brewery is the granddaddy of them all. They've been a Bend and Northwest staple for 30 years and have played an important role in helping other local and regional breweries start and grow. Deschutes' employees love their employer and so do the people of Bend. *deschutesbrewery.com.*

Economic Development for Central Oregon (EDCO): EDCO is the guiding light of Bend's new economy sector and the mother of Pub Talks and Bend Venture Conference. Operating as a 501(c)(6) nonprofit, EDCO's Venture Catalyst has played a leading role in the growth of the tech sector. EDCO creates jobs in two ways: 1) by bringing new businesses to town and 2) by helping those businesses that are already here. *edcoinfo.com.*

Miller Lumber: If your Bend home has been built in the last 107 years, it probably has some Miller wood products in it. Charlie Miller, the owner and CEO of Bend's oldest business, is a third generation Bendite, involved patron of Central Oregon Community College, and an active philanthropist and contributing citizen. *mlumber.com*.

OSU-Cascades: While OSU-Cascades has been delivering higher education to Central Oregon since 2001, its long-awaited, full-fledged, Bend-based campus arrived in 2016. This updated version of OSU-Cascades is the final building block in Bend's educational landscape, allowing Central Oregon students to work and study while living at home. In addition, OSU-Cascades brings an aura of innovation and a sense of academia to Bend's culture. *osucascades.edu*.

Visit Bend: If you're traveling to Bend, Visit Bend should be your first stop—whatever's going on in Bend, they know about it. The driver of Bend's tourism industry through its wide range of marketing programs, Visit Bend also advocates for our sustainable growth, for the maintenance of our caring and friendly community culture, and for the protection of our unmatched outdoor assets. *visitbend.com*.

WHY THIS BOOK?

First and foremost, this book is intended to inspire the people of Bend, both those who currently live here and those who are considering relocating here, to discover their role in our community. I've been fostering this concept of people working together since 1996, when I started Opportunity Knocks (OK), a peer-to-peer, business assistance organization. I'm a believer that there is a price we pay to be a citizen of Bend (or any community for that matter), and that the more people that get involved, the stronger the community becomes. This book is a natural progression of what I learned from OK.

As you read, please remember that *What Makes Bend Special* is largely an "opinion piece," an editorial view of our community through one person's eyes: mine. Since I've been an active participant in our business and nonprofit sectors for the 24 years I've lived in Bend, my opinions have been formed by witnessing many of Bend's outstanding achievements.

After coming up with the idea for this book, I pitched it to the Bend Chamber president, and she pounced on it as a key component of their "Welcome to Bend" package for prospective new businesses and citizens. That's because, she believes, the book will serve as a primer on Bend, providing a backstory to our new citizens and businesses about what makes us tick.

Since I began working on the book, a number of Bend citizens I spoke with also expressed the hope that this book would help preserve Bend's small-town, warm and caring culture as we blast past the 100,000-population mark and spread our wings. Those people don't want Bend to lose the magic that got us here.

This book, then, is intended to 1) welcome some of you to our special community, 2) motivate you and others to get involved, and 3) help protect our small-town culture. If any of these three reasons resonate with you, this book is in the right hands.

Jim Schell

TABLE OF CONTENTS

CHAPTER ONE

WELCOME TO BEND

Welcome to Bend, Oregon, one of the West Coast's finest places to live. Wait, did I say West Coast? How about one of the USA's finest? Ripe for discussion, if you ask me.

For those of us who are Bend old-timers (defined as anyone who has lived here for more than ten years), it's easy to understand why 4,000+ lucky people choose to move here every year. After all, Bend is glitzy (except that our version of glitz is our lifestyle, not our nightlife). That lifestyle is mostly outdoors, where the sun usually shines. From skiing to hiking, kayaking to rafting, mountain biking to rock climbing, fishing to golf, you name the outdoor experience and we've got it covered.

While we're widely known for our outdoor playground, that's only a part of what makes Bend special. What really makes us special is the people who live here, those folks who've turned our playground into the living, breathing, innovative, entrepreneurial, collaborative, joyful community that Bend is.

In the event that you don't live here but are kicking our tires, you should know that there's a responsibility one assumes when moving to Bend—a responsibility that goes beyond entering our roundabouts gracefully, laying off the horn when another car crowds our lane, or ceding space to the squadrons of cyclists that share our streets. That responsibility includes being part of a warm, caring, and respectful community. It's taken a lifetime to create our culture, and we don't want to lose it.

I've witnessed Bend's mercurial growth since moving here in 1994. During the intervening years, I've viewed firsthand the tide of change that has been caused by the growth of our community. Some of that change has been smooth and immediate, other change has been rocky and slow. But things have definitely changed, and, for the most part, Bend is better off for it. (Note: There are plenty of Bend old-timers who would disagree with this statement.) When we (my wife, Mary, and I) arrived in Bend, there were 30,000 hardy souls residing here. As of 2018, there are 95,000, with conservative projections of 125,000 by 2030. Imagine: we'll have added almost 100,000 people to our community in just 36 years! No wonder we've had growing pains along the way. (We'll talk more about those pains later on.)

Since relocating here, I've intersected, in one way or another, with each of the five sectors that make up every community: 1) business, 2) nonprofit, 3) education, 4) faith-based, and 5) government. Over those years, I've learned that it takes a village to make a village, and we owe the vibrancy of Bend to the contributions of people from each of those sectors. For more on those five sectors, see chapters six through ten. With an eye on helping to make Bend even more special than it already is, I've concluded those chapters with suggestions on how you can get involved.

Finally, for those of you who are considering relocating here, there's a Midwestern flavor to Bend's culture that you should know about. (I'm a native Iowan, so I know Midwestern when I see it.) We play hard, we work hard, and we have opinions—boy, do we ever. But our opinions don't stand in the way of solving our problems. When a decision is reached, whether we agree with it or not, we take our hands out of our pockets and we get the work done.

Thanks for sticking with me this far. Now, let's take a closer look at where Bend came from and where it is today.

CHAPTER TWO

A SNAPSHOT OF BEND: THEN AND NOW

"Bend Sucks. Don't Move Here."

So reads a tongue-in-cheek bumper sticker you're likely to catch a glimpse of on a Bend street. The owner of the car bearing that message wants you to know that he thinks Bend is growing too fast and would prefer every outsider who reads it to stay right where they are. This stay-away advice is an updated version of past governor of Oregon Tom McCall's sentiment, who, when referring to tourism in a 1971 speech, uttered his now famous words, "Come visit, don't stay." Back then, there was a frequently stated desire to keep Oregon secret.

Bend was initially incorporated as a city in 1905. For years, Bend was known as "Farewell Bend" by its pioneers because there was a fordable spot across the Deschutes River at this point. After some discussion, the U.S. Post Office approved the name "Bend" over the requested Farewell Bend. Bend, they said, was shorter.

Bend's first sawmill opened in 1903, and until the late 1980s, Bend was primarily a logging town—sometimes rowdy at nights, but excessive growth was never a problem. Bend was not "discovered" by tourists and retirees until the early '90s. Since then, Bend has been exposed in the media as an ideal place to raise a family, to play in the great outdoors, and to embrace Oregon's rugged pioneer mentality that says, "I'd rather do it my way." Bend has had its share of speedbumps and controversies along the way, including the endangered spotted owl, the demise of the logging industry, and the 2008 Great Recession. However, our fair city has worked its way through its difficulties and differences, and has grown bigger and stronger in the process.

The Bend of Today

Today, tourism has replaced logging as Bend's number one industry. Mt. Bachelor, the Cascade Lakes, and the Deschutes River bring tourists by the thousands to Bend. Bend's downtown, with its cute shops, on-trend restaurants, and cool hotels, has been a continuing draw. The iconic Brooks-Scanlon sawmill, the remnants of which are the three smoke stacks you see as you're driving the Parkway, was shut down long ago and has since been replaced by the Old Mill District, yet another draw for tourists, shoppers, and concertgoers. Bend's warm, no-humidity, almost-insect-free summer weather creates the perfect scenario for visitors to enjoy. Bend has also become a popular retirement destination; Broken Top, Mountain High, and Tetherow are examples of neighborhoods created largely for active retirees. At last count there were 25 golf courses within a 30-mile radius of Bend.

The most relentless growth in Bend, however, does not come from retirees. Rather, it comes as a result of the success of our "New Economy" business sector. Chapter six will explain this in more detail, but our New Economy primarily includes technology, bioscience, and outdoor businesses (businesses that cater to outdoor recreation). Entrepreneurs have determined that Bend is a great place to do business and lead lives. Also, New Economy businesses have allowed an enormous number of people to work remotely in Bend. The influx of business people and their families is what drives Bend's innovation and energy, while at the same time contributing to our ongoing need for more affordable housing and more schools.

Despite Bend's steady and sometimes frenetic growth, key elements of our small-town culture remain secure. I was reminded of this on the way to an appointment recently. As I approached a roundabout on a busy eastside Bend street, I noticed a car parked on the curb, its lights flashing. Standing behind the car was a woman, obviously distraught. She was covering her face with her hands; at her feet lay a cat she had accidentally hit.

Suddenly, a car pulled to the curb on the other side of the street. The door opened and another woman rushed across the street, her arms outstretched. There was no conversation. The two women were obviously strangers, but there, as the line of traffic inched by, they hugged. And they hugged.

For me, it was a sad but reassuring scene, yet another example that Bend's caring culture is alive and well. I see examples of it often, in our streets, in our offices, in our public places.

I'm happy to say there is still a pervasive sentiment of caring for our neighbors that is alive and well in Bend. Plenty of our existing citizens are working hard to see that it stays that way. We ask that our newly arrived residents do the same.

CHAPTER 3

BEND'S REPUTATION: HOW OTHERS SEE US

If, as they say, it takes a village to make a village, then that village must be made up of people who work together, play together, and care together. When a community grows at a rapid pace beyond what takes place organically, newcomers must be a part of the mix. Which is what has happened in Bend; over the last two decades, tens of thousands of talented and energetic new residents have relocated here from places around the country, a trend that shows no signs of letting up.

Small wonder that new people are attracted to Bend. Where else can you ski in the morning and play golf in the afternoon? Or play hockey in the morning and go whitewater surfing in the afternoon? Or enjoy world-class rock climbing in the morning and world-class pub hopping in the afternoon? Bend offers its residents a diversified landscape of activities, in the process attracting the kind of people who are used to playing hard and working hard.

No Longer a Secret

In 1994, when I moved to Bend, few people outside of Oregon knew the secret that was Bend; our ascension as a tourist town was still in its formative stages. Over the last two decades, however, the word has leaked out—no, make that spilled out—that Bend is an ultra-cool place to visit. And to live.

Here are a few examples of those words that have spilled out, in the form of Bend being named...

- One of America's 10 best destinations for outdoor enthusiasts (*USA Today*)
- One of the top 52 destinations in the world to visit (*The New York Times*)
- One of the 10 best towns in America (Matador Network)
- One of the 15 U.S. cities with the best restaurant scene (*HuffPost*)
- One of the nation's top beer towns, cycling towns, and ski towns (*USA Today*)
- Best multi-sport town in the U.S. (*Outside* magazine)
- Mountain biking capital of Oregon (**singletracks.com**)
- One of the top 10 mountain biking towns in the U.S. (*National Geographic Adventure* magazine)
- One of the top 12 ski areas in North America (**destinationluxury.com**)
- Birthplace of sport climbing (*USA Climbing*)
- One of the best home base cities for adventure enthusiasts. (**livability.com**)
- The world's best SUP (standup paddleboarding) getaway (*Outside* magazine)
- One of the nation's top five equestrian communities (**equitreking.com**)
- One of the top 10 fly fishing towns in the U.S. (Fly Fisherman)
- The country's No. 1 town for sportsmen (*Outdoor Life*)
- One of the nation's coziest mountain towns (*Harper's Bazaar*)
- America's top adventure town (*Men's Health*)
- No. 4 top trending travel spot in the U.S. (*Trip Advisor*)
- One of 11 epic vacation destinations for adrenaline junkies (*Reader's Digest*)

- One of six unforgettable adventure vacations (*Men's Health*)
- One of America's most romantic cities (**livability.com**)

There are probably more, but you get the point. In terms of an outdoor playground, Bend just about has it all.

Reasons Why Some People Move to Bend

In addition to Bend's outdoor offerings, there are several other reasons why so many people choose to relocate here every year. You'll find Bend right up your alley if you're into...

Dogs: *Dog Fancy* magazine dubbed Bend as Dog Town USA in 2012. Thirteen off-leash parks and endless miles of national forest offer Bend's dogs an expanded world to run, sniff, and chase critters in. OK, so don't get me wrong, you cat lovers, there are plenty of them too. They're just not as loud.

Beer: Bend has more microbreweries per capita than any other Oregon community; at last count we had 25 to choose from. A tour of some of the key microbreweries in town has been dubbed the Bend Ale Trail, providing a popular activity for tourists and natives alike. You can take the Ale Trail tour by bus, by bike, by cycle pub (a pedal-powered mobile bar), by horse-drawn carriage, or by foot.

Cannabis: For those with sore, uh, joints, there's some good news. At last count there were 22 cannabis dispensaries in Bend. In addition to those retail shops, there is also a robust cannabis growing and processing industry in Bend. Whether you're a cannabis fan or not, the industry is here to stay and will only become more impactful to Bend's economy as time goes by. There are also financial benefits to moving to

Bend. While our real estate prices are high relative to much of Oregon, they certainly are more affordable when compared to Seattle, San Francisco, and L.A. Oregon also has no sales tax, which means that when you purchase a $40,000 car you can save up to $3,200.

The best bonus of all could be our weather, especially if you're into seasons. In the summer, our low-humidity, sun-drenched, 85-degree days bestow a climate as pleasant as weather can be anywhere in the world. As a result, there are events practically every weekend from June through early October. In the spring there's the Pole Pedal Paddle and TEDxBend. In the summer there's the Cascade Relays, Munch & Music, the Bite of Bend, Bend Brewfest, and the Fourth of July Pet Parade. In the fall there's Octoberfest and the Bend Venture Conference, and in the winter the Oregon Winterfest, not to mention all kinds of ski events at Mt. Bachelor. (More on our endless menu of events in appendix B.)

In short, no matter the season, you'll never have a problem finding things to do or places to go.

CHAPTER 4

BEND'S OOMPH: TALENT, ENERGY, AND COLLABORATION

The character and culture of any organization is in direct proportion to the kind of people that make it up. Those people include both its leadership and its workforce, and this axiom applies to all organizations, be they public or private. The United States is the sum of its people and so are the state of Oregon, Deschutes County, the City of Bend, St. Charles Hospital, the Bend-La Pine School District, and your neighborhood coffee shop.

The sum of an organization's people isn't just about pure numbers. Rather, it's also about the combined talent of the people that make up those numbers. And it's about the energy those talented people generate in pursuing the work they do. And finally, it's about how those talented and energetic people collaborate.

Talent, energy, and collaboration—here's how the three of them interact...

Talent

Bend has talent, that's for sure. The reason for so much talent in such a small community is that Bend seems to attract the kind of people who are adventurous, entrepreneurial, and motivated to succeed. The people who live in Bend *want* to be here; they have deliberately *chosen* Bend; we've made the well-thought-out cut. They haven't been transferred here, they've come on their own volition. As a result, once they're here they come to care deeply about our community and want to preserve and protect the reasons why they came here in the first place.

Bend's "talent" pool comes from four different demographics. To understand those demographics one must first understand the difference between our "Traditional" and "New Economy" business sectors. Bend's Traditional businesses include those businesses whose services and products are consumed locally and were responsible for getting Bend to where it is today. They trade products, services, and cash within the local economy and include our banks, developers, newspapers, car dealers, utilities, attorneys, CPAs, etc.

Meanwhile, our New Economy sector includes those businesses that (with a couple of exceptions) are relatively new to the community and whose primary customers reside somewhere outside of our region. Sometimes called "traded sector" businesses by the economic development folks, they include industry verticals, such as technology, bioscience, the outdoors, aviation, and food. Examples of New Economy businesses include Hydro Flask, G5, Five Talent, GL Solutions, Cairn, Ruffwear, and Humm Kombucha. Businesses such as these create net cash inflows to our community and to our region.

A key differentiator between Traditional and New Economy businesses is that while Traditional businesses typically grow at the pace of the local population, the pace of growth for New Economy businesses is limited only by their ability to compete in the wider world. Within Bend's ecosystem, there are often New Economy businesses whose revenues grow dramatically from one year to the next, a situation that would be extremely rare for a Traditional business. Thus, the inordinate growth of Bend's business sector has come largely from its New Economy businesses.

The people that make up the Traditional sector are Bend's original architects and leaders, those folks who played a role in designing and creating Bend's infrastructure. They were, and in many cases still are, the people responsible for laying the foundation for the city we enjoy today.

Most of those original architects and leaders came from the business community and include several developers, an attorney, a newspaper publisher, and a bank president, among others. There were also doctors, mayors, a couple of CEOs, a state senator, and a nun. (Yes, a nun. Sister Catherine Hellmann was the driving force behind the founding of St. Charles Hospital.) Check out appendix A for the names of some of those contributors and the extraordinary gifts they've passed on to Bend.

The second demographic of talent is a younger version of the Traditional sector players. These are the men and women who are often second and third generation Bendites, who want to pick up where their predecessors left off. All of them are a younger version of Bend's Traditional business population, and include a developer, several business owners, a contractor, and a gaggle of Bendites who are poised to take the place of yesterday's Traditional leaders.

The third demographic is Bend's potential (but not yet emerging) leaders: the owners, CEOs, and managers of Bend's New Economy businesses. The majority of these folks (including most of Bend's remote workers) are young, have families, and work long hours, meaning they don't have the inclination or time to spend on community betterment. They are a talented, innovative, and energetic group, however, and within the next decade or so some are sure to cross over and get involved. Several have already made the leap.

The fourth demographic is Bend's retired population, those people who have "been there and done that." Some are Bend natives and have had a lifelong love for our community. Others are transplants and have done their high achieving somewhere else. Both have the time and skills to make a difference and some would like to get involved but are not sure what to do or where to look. (This book to the rescue?)

Several local organizations are hard at work looking for ways to assist that retired demographic in finding the right place to become involved. These organizations include Bend's Chamber of Commerce, EDCO (Economic Development for Central Oregon), Looking Forward (*lookingforwardoregon.org*), and Volunteer Central Oregon powered by Better Together. (*volunteerconnectnow.org*).

Energy

In the early 2000s I was hired by the state of Oregon to start chapters of Opportunity Knocks (OK) in eight Oregon communities. OK, founded in 1996, is a peer mentorship organization designed to help business owners, entrepreneurs, and executives (see *opp-knocks.org*) In the process of fulfilling the contract, I learned what made each of those eight communities tick.

Or not.

My job entailed working with half a dozen or so organizations in each community, including its local SBDC (Small Business Development Center), Chamber of Commerce, a bank (usually), the city government (sometimes), and one or two of the community's business leaders. I spent two years traveling the state and getting to know the people in each community who could play a role in successfully completing the OK project. When the project was completed, I had a hands-on knowledge of the character and culture of each of those eight communities.

How is it, I wondered, that communities within the same state have such different results when it comes to developing a robust economy? What made one community perform better than the others?

The biggest difference I witnessed between other Oregon cities and Bend was the energy level. We seemed to have an unmatched reservoir of energy at the time I visited the eight communities; you could see it, feel it, and, most of all, feed off it. I was always re-energized upon returning to Bend and diving back into its high-octane energy.

I'm sure things have changed in those eight communities over the years, just as they've changed in Bend. Today, thanks to the dazzling rise of Bend's New Economy business sector, our energy level is exponentially greater than it was back then. For example, we now have a half-dozen co-working spaces in and around Bend (where small businesses and nonprofit entrepreneurs work side by side with their peers in an open-office environment). We have two Makers Spaces, where people with science and technology skills gather to tinker and create. Walk into any Bend coffee shop and you'll see pockets of men and women wired for sound while hunched over their computers. Examples of Bend's energy can be found everywhere.

You can also see and feel Bend's energy at a wide range of our community and business events. These events include TEDx-Bend, the Bend Venture Conference, Pub Talks, Pole Pedal Paddle, Cascade Relays, and BendFilm. (For more info about Bend's events, see appendix B.)

Bend's bias for energy—as is the case in many communities—starts with the business sector and translates into job creation, which, in turn, serves to energize the entire community. That energy then ripples outward to families, schools, churches, non-profits, organizations, and clubs. This bias in Bend is tangible and relentless; it's at work every day and, from my viewpoint anyway, shows no signs of letting up. Our energy also plays an integral part in the innovative culture we'll talk about in the following chapter.

Collaboration

It's one thing to have talent and energy, but what happens if talent and energy are tugging in different directions? What happens if they compete? What happens if talent trumps energy, or vice versa?

Then talent and energy won't matter, that's what happens. As a matter of fact, if the two are working against each other, they'll make matters worse.

In Bend, talent and energy are aligned. Talent spurs energy and energy abets talent, thanks to a robust culture of collaboration. Which means, as they say, Bend's whole is greater than the sum of its parts.

What Organizations Work to Promote Collaboration?

Following is a partial list of those organizations that have set the pace for Bend becoming as collaborative as it is today.

EDCO: In 1999, with the arrival of Roger Lee as its newly hired Executive Director, EDCO (Economic Development for Central

Oregon) began fostering a culture of collaboration between all of the organizations that serve Bend's business community. Today, EDCO collaborates with everyone, including Bend's Chamber of Commerce, the City of Bend, and the three counties in our region (all of whom, in return, partially fund ED-CO's existence). EDCO also actively collaborates with our education sector (Bend-La Pine School District, OSU-Cascades, and COCC), our region's service providers (all of the Chambers of Commerce), and with dozens, if not hundreds, of our local business leaders and innovators. They also collaborate with our two tourism agencies, Visit Bend and COVA (Central Oregon Visitors Association).

Bend Chamber of Commerce: The Bend Chamber is an active collaborator as well. Today, the Chamber has adopted a "compromise and collaborate" approach to resolving the conflicting issues that naturally emerge in rapidly changing environments. In 2017, the Chamber launched, in partnership with the education sector, a much-needed, community-wide, internship program for high school and college students, in effect aligning the business community's needs with Bend's education providers. It was a welcome and timely collaboration, if ever there was one.

Opportunity Knocks: When OK was founded in 1996, it initiated the concept of collaboration between peers, i.e., Bend's entrepreneurs helping each other. As described earlier, OK creates an environment for peers to share their best practices and help each other solve their problems. The result is a highly collaborative environment of people helping people.

Bend-La Pine School District: Thanks to an innovative and enlightened staff, the BLSD actively collaborates with Bend's private and public sectors. Ditto with OSU-Cascades and COCC (Central Oregon Community College). The level of collaboration within our education sector is extraordinary, the result of which spells excellent news for the future of our kids and our home-bred workforce.

OSU-Cascades: OSU-Cascades collaborates with the business community in many ways, including creating opportunities for its students to intern with Bend businesses. Also, its Innovation Co-Lab offers a wide range of training opportunities for business owners. OSU-Cascades also actively participates in supporting Bend's culture, including taking the lead sponsorship in such events as TEDxBend.

City Club of Central Oregon: A Bend-based nonprofit, the City Club, whose tagline is "Conversation Creates Community," offers monthly luncheons designed to promote community-wide conversations on current topics. Topics include issues that impact Bend and our region and range from transportation to immigration to Bend's housing issues and growth.

Central Oregon Association of Realtors and the Central Oregon Builders Association: COAR (1900 members) and COBA (600 members) regularly collaborate with each other as well as with the Bend Chamber (1,200 members) and with EDCO (400 members). These are hefty membership numbers for a community and region of our size. There is strength in numbers and the inclination these two organizations have shown toward working together and benefiting our community has been substantial.

At Heart, Bend is Still a Small Town

Despite our growing population, Bend still has a distinctive small-town flavor, which means that most of our organizational and sector leaders are on a first-name basis with each other, accounting for their penchant to put the needs of the community above the needs of their sector. Turf issues, at an organizational level anyway, certainly exist but are not of lasting, impactful significance. Today, serving Bend's greater good seems to be most key leaders' goal.

Those people who are involved in Bend's infrastructure are quick to agree that our community has an unusually collaborative culture. Studies show that organizations (or people) who are highly collaborative are also highly innovative. Thus, Bend's collaboration and innovation run hand in hand; one begets the other.

The formula, then, for what makes Bend's whole greater than the sum of its parts, is...

Talent + Energy + Collaboration = Innovation

Jim Collins must have been thinking of Bend when he wrote his seminal book, *Good to Great*. "When the right people are on the bus and in the right seats," he wrote, "good things result."

The Bend of today is the culmination of our bus-driving leaders convening at the right bus stop in the first place.

CHAPTER 5

THE OUTCOME OF BEND'S COLLABORATIVE CULTURE: INNOVATION

In the previous chapter we talked about people who are highly collaborative also being innovative. Given Bend's collaborative culture, it's not surprising that innovation plays such an important role in Bend's infrastructure.

Bend's high degree of innovation has not gone unnoticed; in the spring of 2017, a swath of Bend's industrial complex was officially designated as an "Innovation District" by our City Council. This was the first step taken by several of our business leaders to designate the entire city of Bend as the "City of Innovation."

The Proof Is Out There

It's one thing to be designated as "innovative," it's something else to actually *be* innovative. After all, innovation is a difficult word to quantify. There's tangible evidence, however, that points to Bend rightfully earning the innovation designation. Here is a sampling of that evidence:

- In January 2018, the Milken Institute's Best-Performing Cities (BPC) U.S. index named the Bend-Redmond metro area as the No. 1 performing small city in the U.S. for 2017. The designation was based on the consistency of economic performance, with 9 different benchmarks used as criteria.

- In 2017 Bend-Redmond ranked No. 1 in the nation in small-community wage growth and No. 2 in job growth.

- In 2017 there was one new business registration for every 28 residents in Bend, the highest ratio in the state for communities over 30,000 people. This compares to Portland at 84 business registrations per resident and a statewide average of 65 per resident. Jobs in Bend's professional, scientific, and technical services have increased 14.6 percent from 2015 to 2016 and 43 percent from 2011 to 2016.

- In 2016 Bend was named the "Best Small City for Business and Careers" by *Forbes* magazine.

In addition to that hard evidence, here's a slice of anecdotal evidence that has cemented—at least for me—the rightfulness of Bend's innovative designation:

In 2014 a friend and I traveled to Boulder, Colorado, and interviewed a dozen or so of the movers and shakers active in their entrepreneurial ecosystem. Boulder was, and still is, widely considered to be one of the more innovative business communities of its size in the U.S. Our goal was to see what best entrepreneurial practices they might have that we could bring back to Bend.

The results of that visit? We learned firsthand that our ecosystem was broader and had more moving parts than their ecosystem. We also learned that we provided more services for those small-business owners who operated outside of the tech sector. By our definition, we learned that Bend's small-business infrastructure back then was more innovative then Boulder's ecosystem.

Where offering an environment for entrepreneurs is concerned (who are the primary drivers of innovation in most communities), we believe we confirmed what *Forbes* and the Milken Institute have since quantified: Bend's business success is due in part to the innovativeness of its entrepreneurial infrastructure.

Bend's History of Innovation

Bend has worked its way through three identifiable stages of innovation in the 25 years since I came to town. The first stage transpired in the early 1990s, set in force by the logging industry's decline and subsequent disappearance. Thankfully, Bend's city fathers made the wise decision to shift gears and transition Bend's industry focus from logging to tourism. That innovative decision resulted in the beginning of an influx of visitors to Bend and the Central Oregon region, which in turn accounted for us being "discovered." In 2017, tourists reportedly spent $903M in Central Oregon, real money in a region with 240,000 residents. More importantly, tourism today accounts for 9,400 jobs in Central Oregon.

The second stage of Bend's innovation took place in the late 1990s. Two of Bend's great visionaries, Mike Hollern and Bill Smith, started the wheels in motion that resulted in the Bend Parkway (Hollern) and the Old Mill District (Smith). The Parkway made travel around and through Bend more scenic and efficient; the Old Mill District expanded our shopping and dining opportunities and attracted national brand stores.

Another significant contributor to innovation's second stage was BendBroadband's introduction of high-speed broadband services. As a result, Bendites enjoy one of the highest broadband penetration rates in the country, a factor that led to our penchant for attracting remote workers. Visitors to Bend in the late 1990s often claimed that they didn't have our internet speeds in San Diego, Orange Country, or Palo Alto.

Bend's third stage of innovation was the surge of our New Economy sector, which began gathering momentum shortly after the Great Recession (2010 or thereabouts). Precipitating the boom was EDCO's receipt of a three-year federal grant to fund a "Venture Catalyst" position, i.e., a person who works hand in hand with Bend's New Economy businesses, especially those in technology.

Today, innovation can be found everywhere in Bend's business community. Our newly-formed cannabis industry is the latest example. The industry, which erupted in Oregon in 2016, went from zero to 60 faster than a Porsche 911. By 2017 we had 22 cannabis stores generating an estimated $25M in revenues and creating 100 (estimated) jobs.

Certainly, there's more to an innovation ecosystem than just the business sector. In addition to business, every community has four other sectors at work—education, government, nonprofit, and faith-based—the five of which contribute to its innovative infrastructure. Thus, a community's degree of innovation is a sum of the contributions from each of these five sectors. While typically it is the business community's entrepreneurs that set the tone for innovation, the opportunity to innovate can be found everywhere.

CHAPTER 6

BEND'S BUSINESS SECTOR: AN UNMATCHED ENTREPRENEURIAL ECOSYSTEM

Wikipedia defines the term "entrepreneurial ecosystem" as "the social and economic environment affecting the local and regional entrepreneurship." Every community has one, whether they call it that or not. An entrepreneurial ecosystem (EE) is made up of business organizations that offer support to entrepreneurs, and could include the Chamber of Commerce, any and all economic development organizations, certain nonprofit and for-profit organizations, and Rotary Clubs. Some communities also may have an ad hoc group of business owners and leaders that meet to discuss and act on issues relating to their entrepreneurs and small-business owners.

As mentioned in the previous chapter, one of the nation's premier entrepreneurial ecosystems is located in Boulder, Colorado. Their EE got an early start, the construction of which began in the early '90s, and has evolved into a vibrant and nationally known ecosystem today. Boulder's business community has many similarities to Bend's, hence our visit there.

Lessons from Boulder

The purpose of that Boulder visit was to determine if they had any best practices within their business community that Bend was missing and could adopt. The number one lesson we learned was illuminating but not surprising; Bend's EE was significantly broader than theirs. For instance, Boulder didn't have a Bend Venture Conference, they didn't have an Opportunity Knocks, and they didn't have a Stable of Experts (a program providing free expertise to business owners). They also didn't have the degree of collaboration that Bend had; their government and business sectors had an unusually adversarial relationship.

What Boulder did have that Bend didn't, however, was depth in the resources they did have. Their largest venture capital fund had $250M in assets at the time while ours had $10M. (Today we have $40M.) Their ecosystem had been in place much longer than ours. Brad Feld instituted theirs beginning in the early '90s, while Roger Lee, Bend's ecosystem designer, didn't come to Bend until 1999.

The development of Bend's EE began when Lee became the executive director of the Economic Development for Central Oregon (EDCO) nonprofit. Thanks to the highly entrepreneurial staff that Lee assembled, Bend's EE began its steady ascent to the lofty level at which it operates today.

Collaboration at Work

Thanks to a number of visionary business people, Bend's business community learned that collaboration is the key to the development of a successful EE. The adaptation of our "cluster system" is an example of how collaboration can result in big dividends for an entrepreneurial ecosystem.

In 2015, EDCO won a federal grant allowing them to create a cluster program in Bend. Thanks to that grant they subsequently created a position called "Cluster Coordinator." The Cluster

Coordinator's duty was to develop and organize "clusters" of businesses within several of Bend's most populated vertical industries. Included in these clusters are businesses in tech, bioscience, outdoor products, aviation, and food. Each of these verticals includes at least a dozen businesses—most have significantly more.

The Cluster Coordinator then invited the business owners and CEOs from those verticals to a facilitated meeting. Those meetings were initially designed to network, trade news and updates, and share best practices. Today, three years later, all five of those clusters have groups of peers that meet regularly and several have hired part-time staff. Collaboration is what makes them work.

Almost all of Bend's cluster businesses are made up of New Economy businesses and much of our EE focuses on those businesses too. Why are New Economy businesses so important to Bend? Because that's where the opportunity for growth exists, and when a business grows, it creates jobs. After all, it is job growth that makes for healthy communities, which means the primary motivation behind Bend developing a robust entrepreneurial ecosystem is not to make millionaires out of our entrepreneurs, but rather to create jobs.

Another example of Bend's interorganizational collaboration comes by way of Deschutes Brewery, Bend's iconic craft beer brewer. Deschutes was the first of what is today an estimated 25 microbreweries throughout Central Oregon. Many of those 25 breweries were started by ex-Deschutes employees. Rather than treat the offshoot breweries as competitors, Deschutes chose to encourage and support them. As a result, Central Oregon has become known as a hub for specialty breweries, which in turn creates tourism, demand for Bend's beer, and a supportive entrepreneurial ecosystem. This example illustrates how Bend's collaborative culture creates far greater community good than Deschutes Brewery's management may have imagined 25 years ago.

Growth-Made Challenges

While Bend's business growth has been exciting, there have been repercussions as a result of that pace; for every action, there is a reaction. One of the most painful repercussions is affordable housing. Bend is currently learning what San Francisco and Boulder have been suffering through for so many years: too little housing plus too much demand results in sky-high housing prices. Our city government is struggling to develop a solution to the housing crisis; meanwhile, the influx of Bend residents shows no signs of letting up.

Another growth-related challenge includes living-wage jobs. Logging jobs paid well; tourism jobs typically do not and many are only seasonal. For a number of years Bend's unofficial tagline was "poverty with a view," a situation that still has too much relevancy today. New Economy jobs, particularly in tech and bioscience, are boosting the number of well-paid jobs (for some, anyway) in Bend. We've made progress in this respect but there is much more to be done. Unfortunately, the issue of income disparity is as concerning in Bend as it is in the rest of the U.S.

Bend's transportation system is also struggling, as it is in all of Central Oregon. Our region's transportation network is overseen and managed by the Central Oregon Intergovernmental Council (COIC), a quasi-government organization that receives its funding from the federal and state government. As this is written, COIC is currently reviewing the existing transportation system—and the vision behind it—with help from Bend 2030 and the City of Bend.

Bend also has its share of homelessness and substance abuse problems. We are, however, fortunate to have a vibrant and collaborative nonprofit community, thus there is a large contingent of qualified people tackling all of our social issues.

Finally, the increased usage of Bend's outdoor resources continues to increase, as a result of so many people moving here or visiting here. This is, however, a natural phenomenon of living in a desirable environment; it is difficult to keep people who enjoy our enviable resources from migrating here, either as a resident of a visitor. This stretching of resources is, unfortunately, an unintended consequence of living in an endowed community like Bend.

There are plenty of opportunities if you wish to get involved in contributing your resources to our business sector, either as an investor, consultant, mentor, or volunteer. Our ecosystem was in part constructed as a result of the efforts of individuals like you, and we can always use more.

How you can get involved:

- Business owner, entrepreneur, or savvy business veteran? Opportunity Knocks welcomes new members and facilitators; it's a great way to get to know the community and learn about doing business in Bend. *opp-knocks.org*.

- Cascade Angel Network needs angel investors. Not only will you invest in local and regional businesses, you'll meet interesting people, both within the angel network and within the businesses they serve. *cascadeangels.com*.

- Venture Capital Experience? Check out Seven Peaks Ventures. *sevenpeaksventures.com*.

- Interested in tech, startups, and/or entrepreneurs? Sign up for Kelly Kearsley's clever, funny, relevant blog at *startupbend.com*.

- Become a SCORE (Service Corps of Retired Executives) volunteer. You'll find no shortage of opportunities to help in Bend. *centraloregon.score.org*.

- Join a Rotary Club. There are three Rotary Clubs operating in Bend. You'll meet interesting people, have fun, and make a difference, all at the same time.

CHAPTER 7

BEND'S EDUCATION SECTOR: INNOVATION ON THE MOVE

Thanks to an informed community, a supportive school board, and an innovative leadership team, the Bend-La Pine School District is on the move—upward. In 2017, Bend's voters approved a $268M bond measure that will provide both a new elementary and high school along with upgrades and maintenance to many of the district's existing facilities. At 18,000 students and counting (the fifth largest school district in the state), our district is constantly being pushed to adapt to relentless student growth.

The focus of the new high school, scheduled to open in 2021 in southeast Bend, will be the creation of enough enrollment capacity to meet the demands of our student growth. However, the school district will also be using part of the funding to start something new and exciting: in the fall of 2018, Bend-La Pine Schools will offer two new high school options for interested students. The school district calls these "choice schools."

The first choice school, Realms High School, will be modeled after the same educational approach and guiding principles that have made Bend's second magnet school, Realms Middle School, a successful and popular experiential learning option over the past 17 years. Realms High School will prepare its students for future leadership roles via a trifecta of creating passion, building skills, and fostering character through its learning-by-doing methodology.

The second choice school, Skyline High School, will combine academic content mastery with collaborative inquiry and creative problem solving to help students develop the skills necessary to carry them through college and a career. Skyline will satisfy the interests, skills, and talents of all students, from the humanities and arts to the sciences and technology. The school will incorporate the best practices of other successful design-thinking schools in the U.S., adapting them to the needs of Bend's culture.

These two new choice schools will be co-located in the Brinson Industrial Park area of northeast Bend for an initial incubation period beginning in the fall of 2018. Their future location will be determined as each program develops and grows.

Bend's innovative approach to education is a bright light in a statewide education environment that needs all the help it can get. Oregon ranks 48th in the U.S. for on-time graduation, with only 75 percent of its students graduating "on time." Meanwhile, Bend's 2017 graduation rates were comfortably ahead of the state's average:

- Summit High School = 92%
- Mountain View High School = 86%
- Bend High School = 83%

The High Desert Education Service District

To understand how Bend's K-12 education system works, one must also be aware of the role of the High Desert Education Service District (HDESD). HDESD is an umbrella organization whose mission, in part, is to support four school districts in Central Oregon: Bend-La Pine, Redmond, Crook County, and Sisters. HDESD's 250 employees provide a wide variety of student and family services and school-related support. The support that HDESD provides that is most visible to outsiders is embodied in three innovative programs and one directorship that they've formed, all of which have been incubated in the last few years:

Better Together: Better Together is an HDESD-sponsored organization whose goal is to positively impact student success by collaborating with the community at large. Such collaboration includes working with the business, nonprofit, and government sectors. In this way, Better Together's programs are designed to leverage the resources of the entire community, not just those in the education sector.

Children's Forest of Central Oregon: Children's Forest takes students out of the classroom and into the forests and deserts that surround Bend. Its mission is to inspire our youth, through connecting with nature, to be stewards of our public lands.

Central Oregon STEM Hub: STEM is an acronym for Science, Technology, Engineering, and Math. The goal of the Central Oregon STEM Hub is to encourage critical thinking and multidisciplinary innovation in Central Oregon students, in the process preparing them for a rapidly changing world.

Director of Innovation: The role of this recently created directorship is to foster and inspire a culture of innovation within the HDESD and the Central Oregon school districts it works with. The director partners with and encourages the staff and teachers of Central Oregon's four school districts to create and develop innovative ideas and programs, and then pulls resources from outside the sector to support those projects and programs.

A recent program of note is the Youth CareerConnect (YCC) initiative facilitated by Better Together and operated by the Bend Chamber of Commerce. YCC is an internship system designed to establish a liaison between Bend's three high schools, OSU-Cascades, COCC, HDESD, and the business community. The goal is to develop a streamlined system that increases meaningful internship opportunities for high school and college students while at the same time creating a robust pipeline of local talent for Bend's future workforce. YCC is a huge win-win for our community.

Bend's K-12 sector up to this point has been good but not great. Our unrelenting population growth and expanding student population have made it difficult for the district's leadership to focus on innovation and creativity. The combination of a visionary and charismatic school superintendent, a "get it done" leadership team, a grounded school board, the innovative bent of HDESD, and a community that believes in its kids (and votes with its pocketbook) promises an even brighter future for Bend's K-12 students.

The Long-Awaited OSU-Cascades

In 2016, OSU-Cascades officially opened its new campus following almost 30 years of dreaming by a committed group of Bendites. (OSU-Cascades had been a two-year school for many years but the new campus brought with it a complete four-year program). Central Oregon students now have the option of graduating from high school, testing the education waters at COCC, and then going on to achieve a four-year degree at OSU while living at home. Degrees in engineering, math, technology, business, and teaching are among the first disciplines to have been launched at OSU-Cascades. As a result, OSU-Cascades is providing Central Oregon with a much-needed pipeline of new grads as well as a much-appreciated talent pool.

A survey of recent OSU-Cascades graduates shows that 70 percent of its graduating seniors would not have gone to college unless OSU-Cascades was located in Bend. Also, 25 percent of the first year's graduates were first in their family to graduate from college. Clearly, OSU-Cascades' opening is providing a tangible benefit to Bend and to our region.

OSU-Cascades' appearance has also provided a boost to Bend's culture of innovation. Thanks in part to its location at the confluence of Century Drive and Colorado Avenue, that section of town has been officially declared by the Bend City Council as Bend's Innovation District.

In addition to its positive impact on Bend's innovation culture, OSU-Cascades is also creating jobs. Along with the staff and construction jobs that came with opening the campus, many graduating seniors participate in capstone projects in collaboration with area businesses and organizations, integrating those ideas and potential new businesses with our local environment.

Notably, a professor-led lab experiment spawned Onboard Dynamics, an entrepreneurial, Bend-based business that utilizes natural gas to power cars and trucks, thereby lowering fuel costs and carbon emissions. If this natural gas technology gains traction, all kinds of good things could happen for the business. Another community asset that has evolved thanks to OSU-Cascades' appearance on the scene is the Innovation Co-Lab, a business incubator and co-working space just down the street from the main campus. OSU-Cascades' new campus also includes the Bend Science Station, a nonprofit that provides after-school science education. In 2017, operating out of a cramped space, the Bend Science Station served 7,000 students.

Central Oregon Community College

Completing the education trifecta is Central Oregon Community College (COCC), Oregon's oldest community college. COCC has, for many years, offered both career training and a pathway to higher education to our region's students. COCC also has a four-building campus in Redmond, including the state-of-the-art Redmond Technology Education Center, and smaller campuses in Prineville and Madras.

COCC offers a wide array of programs, from two-year associate degrees and career and technical education to continuing education and community learning classes. COCC's Bend campus also hosts the Small Business Development Center, offering business management advice and assistance to Central Oregon businesses.

Preparing our kids for adulthood is not the only function of Bend's education sector. Here's an interesting education-based anecdote with an economic development ending:

> I have an extremely talented friend—let's call her Julie— who moved to Bend from Philadelphia in 2009. The reason she chose to relocate here? Realms Middle School.

> Julie decided she wanted something more for her two kids (ages nine and seven) than Philadelphia could offer. After lighting up Google for several days, she stumbled on an education alternative offered by Realms School in far-away Bend, Oregon. She'd never heard of Bend but was intrigued by the Realms story and concept. Her adventurous daughter was intrigued too, so they completed the application form and somehow her daughter was accepted, despite the fact that the waiting list for Realms has always numbered in the hundreds, whereupon mother, daughter, and son packed their bags and moved to Bend.

There are no numbers available on how many people choose to relocate to Bend for the quality of its education, but you can bet your high school diploma that when families with kids make the decision to come here, they've researched the quality of our schools. How could they not?

Bend's education system as an economic driver? You bet. Similar to healthcare, it plays an integral role in Bend's infrastructure, which in turn leads to people choosing to relocate, and stay, here.

In the last five years, thanks to the addition of OSU-Cascades, the new vision for the Bend-La Pine School District, and the innovative bent of HDESD, Bend's education sector has taken a giant leap forward. The best, it seems, is yet to come.

How you can get involved:

- Business or individual? Support the Youth CareerConnect program. Talk to the Bend Chamber about how you can get involved. Contact David Haines: *david@bendchamber.org*.

- Take part in your child's school's PTA.

- Interested in supporting innovation in the education sector with time, talent, and/or financial support? Connect with Anna Higgins of HDESD: *innovation@hdesd.org*.

- Consider volunteering in one of the school's Career Education Centers—to help students explore possible careers and higher-education options. *bend.k12.org*.

- Volunteer for FAN (Family Access Network), which connects at-risk students and their families with social services, love, and support. *familyaccessnetwork.org*.

- Investigate the Bend Education Foundation, a fundraising nonprofit, which is the funding arm to the Bend-La pine high school system.

CHAPTER 8

BEND'S NONPROFIT SECTOR: YOU NAME IT, THEY'VE GOT IT COVERED

The majority of Bend's nonprofits are organizations that deliver a wide variety of social services to Bend and the Central Oregon region. Recently, a group of executive directors and leaders of social service nonprofits (in the course of an Opportunity Knocks team meeting) discussed issues common to their sector. Here are several gems that came out of that conversation:

- "The degree of collaboration in the Central Oregon nonprofit community is unlike anything I've ever seen," said a recently-relocated-to-Bend executive director.

- "Maybe it's because, after Bend nearly collapsed in the late '80s, we learned we'd have to cooperate to survive," said a longtime executive director. "Somehow the idea of cooperation over competition took hold and it has never left."

- Another ED noted that the Pacific Northwest's foundations viewed Central Oregon's nonprofits as a "progressive beacon" in rural America. "Our community is willing to try things that other communities would shun," she concluded.

- One ED pointed out the large number of volunteers that work in the sector. "It's kind of a cultural thing," the ED noted. "If you are going to set out to make a difference in Bend, it starts by volunteering for a nonprofit."

These are telling observations, and to most informed community members come as no surprise. It is a well-known fact among those who have a finger on the social-service pulse (such as United Way and our City and County governments) that the contribution our nonprofit organizations make to Bend's and Central Oregon's well-being is extraordinary. This recognition is especially important to those who are part of our donor and philanthropic community; it gives them peace of mind knowing that their donations will be effectively managed. In the last 15 years or so, nonprofits nationwide have learned the hard way that local, state, and federal governments tend to provide less and less financial support for social services. As a result, today's successful nonprofits must depend more and more on the altruism of the local philanthropic community along with local and state foundations.

United Way's Viewpoint

The man who understands Bend's social service sector better than anyone else is Ken Wilhelm, a 30-year veteran of managing and overseeing Bend's United Way. In 2017 his organization collected $1.5M in donations to be distributed to 20 nonprofits that the United Way board of directors deems most worthy. To determine those 20, United Way must be familiar with the entire Central Oregon nonprofit universe, not just the 20 recipients. Which means United Way has an unmatched 30,000-foot view of Bend's, and our region's, nonprofit landscape.

"By far, it's the sense of collaboration between our agencies," Wilhelm said when asked what makes our local nonprofits so innovative and unique. "There is also a minimum of duplication and overlap. As a result of the nonprofit sector's innovative efficiencies, the pressure on our local, state, and federal governments to provide social services has been minimized."

Ken estimates that there are roughly 80 healthy nonprofits actively providing social services in Bend today. Additionally, he believes, there are another 50 or so animal, environmental, economic development, social justice, and civil rights organizations. Not to mention the dozens of nonprofits that serve kids' sports and club activities.

Most, if not all, of the larger social service nonprofits serve all of the communities in the three-county Central Oregon region, not just Bend. The largest of the social service nonprofits (excluding St. Charles Hospital) is Mosaic Medical, with an (approximate) $30M budget. Mosaic has community health centers throughout the region providing medical, dental, and mental health services to patients regardless of income or insurance. The second largest is NeighborImpact, with an approximate budget of $20M. NeighborImpact provides a wide array of services, including food banks, housing assistance, education (Head Start), and heating and energy services. Both Mosaic and NeighborImpact have talented and experienced executive directors and a history of fostering innovation and collaboration inside and outside of their organizations.

Visit Bend is our local tourism nonprofit and another active collaborator. They are also a prime example of how our economic development nonprofits work together; their list of partners range from local governments (City of Bend and Deschutes County) to other economic development nonprofits (EDCO and the Bend Chamber) to the hundreds of Bend businesses that cater to our visiting tourists.

The lesson our nonprofits have all learned? Pragmatic collaboration between related parties results in better services and economics for all.

The Role of St. Charles Health System

Did you know that St. Charles Hospital is a nonprofit too? As such, it turns away no one based on their ability to pay. It's also the region's largest employer—nonprofit or for-profit—with 4,100 employees, which makes it the 600-pound gorilla of Bend's nonprofit sector.

There's a reason a significant percentage of the never-ending stream of retirees who land in Bend have made the decision to relocate here: the St. Charles network of hospitals and the quality of care they provide. Healthcare quality is a must for all age groups, but it's a gamebreaker for those who have seen more sunsets than the rest of the population. St. Charles' reputation for quality care is well deserved, without it Bend (and the region) would never have experienced the degree of growth we've enjoyed.

As this is written, St. Charles is navigating the slings and arrows of the ever-changing healthcare reimbursement system and, as a result, is experiencing budgetary issues that are constricting its ability to grow—but not its ability to provide quality service. While the hospital system currently utilizes a lean operating model (a model designed to result in efficient operations and expense management), the vagaries of the nation's healthcare system have resulted in all kinds of budgetary potholes. St. Charles is not alone; most U.S. hospitals have similar problems.

Recreation and Environmental Protection Nonprofits

Life in a far west, small town is complicated. Recreational interests are often at odds with environmental protection. Access to public lands—for skiing, hiking, and snowmobiling, for example—means both enjoying the resources available while at the same time encroaching on nature. Utilizing our environment includes managing such complicated activities as water usage, protecting streams, and preserving wildlife and their habitats in perpetuity. Not to mention managing water rights, cattle grazing, wilderness areas, habitats, solar and wind power, trail etiquette, and carbon footprints. The list is endless.

Bend has dozens of nonprofits, associations, and clubs that focus on these and other outdoor issues. Examples include...

Bend's Environmental Center is a nonprofit that seeks to engage and educate people interested in the outdoors. Its downtown Bend location makes it easy to pop in and learn what they do.

The Central Oregon Trail Alliance (COTA) collaborates with volunteers, bike shops, the **U.S. Forest Service,** and the **Bureau of Land Management (BLM)** to educate users of our public lands, clear and develop trails, and create cooperation among snowmobilers, skiers, bike riders, dogs, and hikers.

Mt. Bachelor Sports Education Foundation and **Bend Endurance Academy** are the two primary winter sports nonprofits in Bend. They're dedicated to giving enthusiastic youth skiers and bikers an opportunity to train and compete at a national and international level.

XC Oregon is a nonprofit that coaches and promotes Nordic skiing for adult master skiers. Every year, U.S. and Canadian national, Olympic, and elite alpine and Nordic ski programs come to train during Mt. Bachelor's lengthy snow season (November through May).

Other nonprofits are involved in such activities or causes as raptor counting, motocross, polo, land trusts, hunting-dog clubs, disc golf, pickleball, rodeo, master gardeners, shooting, gravel riders, and fly fishing. You name it and if it's done outside, there's a nonprofit for it.

Even the government gets into the act of providing a place for us to play. The U.S. Forest Service manages the land that includes Mt. Bachelor, Phil's Trail, and dozens of forest trailheads and trails. ODOT manages the snow parks and the winter plowing necessary to provide access to Mt. Bachelor. BLM manages the thousands of square miles of rangeland and habitats that we play on and in. This special place we call Bend would not be as special without them.

Where Our Nonprofits Need Help

Is there room for improvement in the nonprofit sector? Isn't there always? The primary key to improving rests in the hands of every nonprofit's board of directors, who are essentially an organized (or occasionally unorganized) collection of volunteers who want to do good things for their community. Bend's nonprofits can always use more qualified board members, and the community badly needs some sort of training program for the ones we have now.

Another key area where nonprofits need help is having access to more on-the-front-lines volunteers. We never seem to have enough.

Oddly enough, the degree of contributions that Bend's nonprofit sector makes to the community is one of our best-kept secrets. Most Bendites have no idea how much we are indebted to them.

How you can get involved:

- Volunteer to serve on a nonprofit board. For general information on the names and services of Bend's social service nonprofits, dial 211 (Central Oregon's help line).

- Volunteer for a nonprofit. This is a great way to try out an organization to see if you are interested in making a bigger time commitment. Check out *volunteerconnectnow.org* for opportunities.

- Write a really big check to your favorite social service nonprofit. If you're unsure which nonprofit that should be, make it out to United Way and let them do the due diligence for you.

- Become an Oregon Community Foundation donor by creating your own charitable fund or by donating to a pooled fund. See *oregoncf.org*.

CHAPTER 9

BEND'S FAITH-BASED SECTOR: MAKING PROGRESS ON THE COLLABORATION FRONT

Bend has a healthy, caring, and involved faith-based sector. Our churches provide a tangible public service, above and beyond providing the spiritual guidance they're known for. They also provide a platform for their congregations to do good work, both in the community and in the outside world. Bend's churches are famous for coalescing their resources and making a difference in whatever local or worldwide social problem they decide to undertake.

In addition to pursuing Bend's known pockets of need, our churches are effective at working outside of the box. Show them an opportunity to find a creative solution to a problem and watch them step up, assemble members of their congregation, and work their magic to get the job done.

While our churches work well within their own congregations, there exists a wide-open opportunity for them to work more closely with each other and, in the process, combine their resources and make an even bigger difference.

Inter-Church Collaboration

Oregon, we're told, is one of the most "unchurched" states in the U.S., right up there with Washington and Vermont. This is due, in part, to the independence of the typical Oregonian, who seeks and finds the spiritual guidance she needs outside of the church.

This spirt of independence manifests itself upward to include the churches themselves. Despite the fact that Bend's other sectors are hugely collaborative, this spirit of working together does not translate to churches. In the interchurch world, collaboration would be a welcome addition.

For reasons that go beyond the purpose of this book, the concept of churches failing to collaborate with one another is not an issue unique to our community, it seems to be true across the U.S. If interested in the topic, google "Why don't churches work together?" and you'll find a number of viewpoints on the topic.

Full disclosure: From 2007-2010, I was a team member of a regional nonprofit whose mission was to reduce poverty. Our MO was to play the lead role in unifying the region's existing social service resources rather than developing new ones. Which meant, where the faith-based sector was concerned, our goal was to try and help our churches work together.

We viewed the faith-based community as a ripe opportunity to improve collaboration, hoping to leverage the strength of the many congregations. After all, who better to do good work than those in the faith-based community? With the opportunity of leveraging such resources on our mind, we developed a program designed to organize the churches in Bend, Redmond, La Pine, Madras, and Prineville into what we called "faith-based networks."

Thanks to the commitment of several key pastors, the faith-based network concept worked like a charm in Madras and Prineville. Ten years later, Madras' and Prineville's faith-based networks still play an important role in their community's social service ecosystem. Meanwhile, our attempt to unify the churches in Bend struggled. The faith-based network that was formed at the outset of the project lasted only a year before grinding to a halt due to a lack of support from the pastors.

Faith-Based Innovation

As of late there have been steps taken in a more collaborative direction. In 2014 Mike Sipe, a member of Westside Church, started a C12 chapter in Bend. C12 is a national, nondenominational, faith-based organization whose mission is "to change the world through the platform of business." C12 is, in effect, a peer advisory board of Christian CEOs. They meet once a month to create and develop nondenominational ways to change the world and their communities.

Sipe is also, along with other community leaders, the organizer of the Community Leaders Prayer Breakfast in Bend, an event where community leaders from all faiths gather to discuss faith-based and societal issues. Mike is a past board member of the Bend Chamber of Commerce and, as this is written, the current president of his Rotary Club, so he's seen firsthand how collaboration can work in the business sector.

One big win from Bend's past, and an example of what can happen when churches do work together, is Bethlehem Inn, Bend's homeless shelter for individuals and families. Bethlehem Inn was originally a faith-based collaboration, the location of which rotated monthly among various churches. Businesses, clubs, and other organizations volunteered for 24-hour shifts to prepare food, intake clients, chat, and enforce rules. This utilization of businesses and private citizens by our churches contributed to a groundswell of emotional and financial support such that Bethlehem Inn is today a successful standalone nonprofit with a permanent shelter. This transition succeeded because church-es, in this instance, not only worked together but brought in other sectors of the community as well.

There are other more recent examples of collaboration at the faith-based level that indicate that things may be changing. Two unique programs began operating in 2017 thanks to multi-church collaboration. One is the Shower Truck program, a proj-ect that outfits trucks with showers for homeless individuals who don't have access to one. The other is the Faith Families program, a joint venture between several churches that offers a much-needed pre-foster care program for children.

There is a new generation of young pastors in Bend who are leading the way in encouraging more collaboration among churches, the trend is definitely upward. That collaboration could take many forms, the most important of which would be coordinating every church's community-wide programs, beef-ing up those programs that fill the greatest needs, and making sure there isn't overlap between them.

How you can get involved:

- Church member? Advocate for your church to collaborate with other churches.

- Non-church member who is looking for a church? Join a church that collaborates with other churches.

- CEO with a strong Christian faith? Become a member of C12. *c12group.com*.

CHAPTER 10

BEND'S GOVERNMENT SECTOR: WORKING HARD TO KEEP UP

If you live in Bend, you fall within the purview of four governments: the City of Bend, Deschutes County, the State of Oregon, and the good ol' U.S. of A. I'll leave it to you to determine whether or not you're getting your money's worth from the state or the feds, but this chapter will give you an overview of your city and county governments.

City of Bend

Eric King, Bend's city manager, has the most difficult job in town. No, make that in Central Oregon. Maybe even in the State of Oregon.

Why? Because Bend just won't stop growing. In 2016 Bend was the sixth fastest-growing community in the U.S. and the number-one fastest-growing community not in the southern U.S.

King's job would be a lot easier if he were the city manager of any number of other Oregon communities, cities where population growth is either flat, down, or sporadic. In that case, he'd only have to worry about maintaining the status quo instead of dealing with the ever-changing demands of a burgeoning community.

The good news about being a city manager in Bend is that you don't have to focus on economic development—EDCO, the Bend

Chamber, Opportunity Knocks, and other business assistance organizations take care of that. The other good news is that, thanks to the New Economy business sector and the investment money that has poured into it, Deschutes County accounted for 20 percent of the State's job growth in 2017 while representing less than 4 percent of its population. The bad news? Eric King does have to worry about everything else, like the endless problems caused by the City's relentless growth, such as affordable housing, transportation, and public safety. Not to mention the urban growth boundary and downtown parking and the potholes caused by Bend's ever-increasing traffic.

Aside from Bend's unswerving growth, the primary reason that the City of Bend has so many challenges is due to the way in which governments must work. Change can't take place overnight thanks to the checks and balances required when dealing with public monies. The pace of democracy is slow; governments aren't designed to turn on a dime. Sometimes not even on a quarter.

An additional challenge is that Bend must work within the context of state laws, many of them unfavorable to fast-growing cities. Most notable is Oregon's antiquated real property system dating back to a statewide constitutional initiative passed in 1990. As a result, the City of Bend is limited in the amount of taxes it can collect, a limit that is especially hurtful to rapidly growing communities. The result is that Bend has had the same tax rate ($2.80 per $1,000 of tax assessed valued property) since 1981 and is unable to change it thanks to the State's constitution. The City must also participate in the State-run Public Employees Retirement System (PERS), which, similar to most government pension systems, is struggling to stay solvent. The result of PERS has been steadily increasing expenses for governments, which in turn erodes their ability to provide critical services.

Additionally, Oregon's land-use system, originally designed to protect its agricultural land, penalizes rapidly growing communities like Bend. Adopted in the 1970s, this process-laden and highly litigious system was designed in a bygone era. Bend's effort to expand its urban growth boundary took nearly ten years and cost $10M.

Oregon's urban growth boundary laws are not all bad, however; they are intended to contain urban sprawl. Visitors see the difference as they drive through farmland between towns rather than contiguous sprawling neighborhoods with connected lots. The creation of higher-density small cities offers the benefits of attractive scenery, locally grown produce and grass-fed livestock, knowing your neighbors, driving less, and controlling your carbon footprint. The primary problem with the UGB process is the time and money required to stumble through the bureaucracy of Oregon's state government.

Here's a quick primer on a few key facts about Bend's government:

1. Bend's annual revenue is about $150M—a third of which is generated from property taxes and pays for things like police and fire. The other two-thirds is generated from fees for services like water, sewer, and development.

2. The City of Bend has seven City Council members, one of whom doubles as the mayor. As of May 2018, the mayor will be elected by the public. Council members serve for four years and are minimally compensated.

3. City Council membership is nonpartisan. The Council includes liberal, moderate, and conservative members, and the balance of power has swayed back and forth over the years.

4. The City of Bend is slightly skewed toward Democrat, but only slightly. 30 percent of Bend voters are independent. That 30 percent typically decides the election.

5. Bend Park & Recreation District is a separate taxing district. They are not part of the city government but have a relatively large budget and broad support from the community.

Remember the story in the business chapter—chapter six—about my visit to Boulder? Well, one thing we noticed during that visit was the degree of conflict between the business sector and Boulder's City Council. The discord between the two sectors was palpable. In the words of one of Boulder's business leaders, "We've given up. We pretend they're not there."

Not so in Bend; our collaborative culture won't allow it. New leadership at the Bend Chamber of Commerce has helped engender the degree of collaboration within the business community. Certainly, there will always be disagreements as the Council floats back and forth between liberal and conservative tendencies, pro-growth and slow-growth preferences, and business-friendly to not-so-friendly ideals.

Yes, city government, with its slow-moving gears, can be frustrating to business owners and certain segments of the general public, but moving too quickly can be dangerous as well. And Bend does always seem to be in a hurry, which means that whatever the city government does can never be done fast enough—yet another unintended consequence of having an active and energetic population.

Deschutes County

At a steady four-percent increase in population a year, Deschutes County is experiencing growth consistent with that of Bend's five-percent. The County's population at the end of 2017 was approximately 185,000, with roughly 95,000 of those people residing in Bend. Where the steady, unending increase in population is concerned, the city and county governments are in lockstep.

The County, with a 2018 annual budget of $356M, provides services such as road maintenance, sheriff, and corrections services. Additionally, it oversees the region's mental healthcare, landfill, and 911 services for its residents, thus, in these cases, serving both city and county residents.

People who have been around Bend for a spell have noticed that the Deschutes County government appears to operate more efficiently, or at least more quietly, than the city. Both are probably true. Here are several reasons why:

1. The decision makers for Deschutes County are three elected officials (aka commissioners) who are paid, full-time employees, often with many years of experience in their positions. Meanwhile, the City Council is the decision maker for the City of Bend and is made up of seven "lay people." Those lay people, who are essentially volunteers, are more difficult to coordinate than three paid staff members.

2. County officials run on a party ticket, City Council members don't. Since Deschutes County is traditionally Republican, partisanship is not as prevalent with the County Commissioners as it is with the City Councilors. As of this writing, all three County Commissioners are Republicans; therefore, the likelihood of agreement on issues is more likely.

3. The county is less visible. Its constituency is spread out and unorganized—no neighborhood associations, for instance. Unlike with the City, county-wide advocacy and politicized groups are rare.

4. The County's flash points seem to be fewer. At this writing, the issue of growing marijuana is the primary flash point for the county, while the City's includes affordable housing, transportation, and, lest I forget, potholes.

The best word to describe the Deschutes County government is "dependable." Most of us can depend on the County to keep our roads plowed in the winter, 911 to be picked up on the first ring, and our landfill open and operating when we need it. The County isn't flashy, but they get the job done. Quietly and (usually) on time.

Bend Parks & Recreation District

Bend Park & Recreation is a separate taxing district, which means don't bother calling the City when you want to know why the grass in your neighborhood park hasn't been mowed. They own/operate 81 parks and open spaces along with maintaining 65 miles of trail.. Bend Park & Rec is governed by a five-member board of directors and is managed by their longtime veteran executive director, Don Horton.

Bend Park & Rec is the envy of our local governments, and not just because their offices have the best views in town. Bend's voters have a history of voting favorably for Park & Rec bonds—witness The Pavilion (our ice rink), Bend Whitewater Park (our surf park), skateboard parks, soccer and lacrosse fields, and neighborhood parks. You name it and Bend's voters have given Park & Rec the money to build it.

Part of the reason Park & Rec gets what they want is because Bend voters came here for the outdoor lifestyle and they want plenty of places to play, which is what Park & Rec is meant to provide.

A second reason is that Bend voters perceive that Park & Rec has been worthy stewards of the money they've been allotted. They've largely done what they've said they would do, with plenty of transparency.

A third reason is that some Park & Rec bonds and initiatives have been active collaborations between citizens, businesses, and Park & Rec. Both The Pavilion and the Whitewater Park were originally grassroots, passion-driven efforts led by groups of individuals, and when it came time to pay for the project, private fundraising efforts helped. Speaking of money, Park & Rec has its own foundation, in the event you want to help finance one of their projects. Think about it: what other government entity do you know of that has a foundation?

Bend's Park & Rec employees are busy people, especially in the summertime. You've met their employees if you've floated the Deschutes River and needed an inner tube or a bus ride back to the starting line. They run sports leagues for kids and adults, summer programs for kids, plenty of classes for retirees, and own and manage the Juniper Swim & Fitness Center. They have countless outdoor and indoor programs for adults and children with disabilities as well as plenty of classes for retirees. The Fourth of July parade? Your ten-year-old wants to learn how to fish? Volunteer opportunities for your teenager? You guessed it, Park & Rec has it.

Besides providing Bend's citizens with all those opportunities to play, Park & Rec is also an important economic development engine. Stop by the endless sports fields at Pine Nursery Park in the summertime and you'll usually find something big going on: a regional Little League tournament, a statewide lacrosse tournament, a West Coast pickleball extravaganza. The participants and their families come from all over the map, and they stay in our hotels and eat in our restaurants and shop in our shops.

Innovations and Opportunities

There have been several interesting innovations that have impacted Bend's government sector in the last decade or so. One is Bend 2030, a 501(c)3 started in 2005 by a group of Bend citizens and designed to "engage the community and help the government make choices and set priorities" for the 25-year span from 2005 to 2030. Bend 2030 had a rocky beginning, largely due to funding problems caused by the Great Recession, but has made a spirited comeback in recent years thanks to more focused leadership in step with community-based financial support.

Another innovative government-related program is the Bend Neighborhood Associations. The City of Bend is divided into 13 neighborhood associations designed to provide residents the opportunity to help shape the future of their neighborhood. Each neighborhood program is funded by a city grant and includes a pipeline by which the 13 associations can work with city staff in getting their problems resolved and their needs met.

There exists in Bend an opportunity for our local governments to pick up on the collaborative spirit that prevails in our business, nonprofit, and education sectors. Opportunities for increased collaboration can be found between the City of Bend and Deschutes County; the City and Park & Rec; Deschutes County and Park & Rec; and the City, county, and education sector.

Here's hoping...

How you can get involved:

- Vote for City Council members who live and understand Bend's culture, and who are likely to make city infrastructural decisions that protect our existing culture.

- Ditto above for Deschutes County commissioner elections.

- Join your neighborhood association. See the City of Bend's website for a listing of those associations. *bendoregon.gov*

- Support Bend 2030. Apply to be a board member, join a committee, or make a financial contribution. *bend2030.org*.

- Volunteer for a City of Bend committee. As of this writing, there are seven standing committees and five ad hocs. Google City of Bend volunteer opportunities.

- Volunteer for a Deschutes County committee. Google Deschutes County volunteer opportunities.

- Attend City Council meetings.

- And, of course, vote, giving special consideration to those candidates who are committed to protecting Bend's culture.

CHAPTER 11

BEND'S ARTS AND CULTURE SCENE: ICING ON THE CAKE

Bend has a broad-based and active arts and culture community, which seems to go hand-in-hand with a town filled with active people. Luckily, there's no reason for us to wonder what's going on in the arts and culture scene—*The Bend Bulletin, Cascade Business News,* and *The Source Weekly* all offer something for those individuals who want to keep tabs on where the action is.

Go! Magazine is *The Bend Bulletin's* entry in the arts and culture news-tracking derby. Sign up online and they will deliver to your inbox—at 2:00 p.m. sharp every Thursday, no less—their updated version of *Go Magazine!,* featuring the current week's arts, entertainment, and events. Check out bendbulletin.com and prepare yourself for another arts-and-culture-fueled weekend.

Then there's *Cascade Arts & Entertainment,* a monthly magazine published by Cascade Publications Inc., which also publishes *Cascade Business News.* Interested in maintaining an updated calendar on what's happening in the arts and culture scene this week? Go to their website *cascadeae.com.*

The Source Weekly completes the trifecta. Billing itself as a weekly arts and culture newspaper, *The Source* also includes an events calendar along with the latest reviews of Bend's rocking music scene and backstories on some of the artists. See *bendsource.*

com. You can pick up the latest issue of *The Source, Bend Magazine* and/or *Cascade Arts & Entertainment* at just about any coffee shop in town.

A hub for Bend's art and culture scene is the uber-collaborative Arts and Culture Alliance of Central Oregon. Talk about collaboration; the Alliance has 50-plus members, including nonprofits, organizations, and individuals. Founded in 2010, its members range from the Sisters Folk Festival (a don't-miss event in a very cool community) to the Central Oregon Symphony to BendFilm.

The Arts and Culture Alliance (*artsandcultureco.org*) is a nonprofit whose mission is to "work together to promote, enhance, and expand arts and culture in Central Oregon." Not only is its membership collaborative, so is its funding, which comes from the state, the three counties of Central Oregon, the City of Bend, and its membership.

In 2018 the position of Creative Laureate was established in the City of Bend, only the second city in Oregon to host such a position (Portland was the first.) Administered by the Alliance, the creative laureate will participate in community education, advocacy, and public events, including speaking engagements and workshops.

Another key contributor to the arts and culture scene is Scale-House (scalehouse.org). Billing itself as a contemporary creative center, ScaleHouse produces year-round talks, workshops, exhibitions, performances, special events, and one of Bend's favorite events, the Bend Design Conference (see appendix D). ScaleHouse delivers its services by utilizing such mediums as the visual arts, performing arts, architecture and design, film and storytelling, and conceptual arts and activism. See *scalehouse.org.*

Sorry, kids, but Bend does not have a zoo. Yet. But we do have a museum, complete with otters, owls, eagles, all kinds of high desert flora and fauna, and natural history exhibits. The High Desert Museum (*highdesertmuseum.org*) was founded in 1982 by the late Donald Kerr, a Bend visionary who saw a need and did what Bendites do when an opportunity presents itself. Today, the museum serves citizens and tourists as well as our K-12 student population, who are frequent visitors to its cultural and natural history exhibits.

The Deschutes Public Library Foundation and COCC can often be found at the center of the arts and entertainment scene. Bend has come to enjoy the internationally renowned authors and scholars that these two organizations bring to our community. Check out dplfoundation.org for an update on the Foundation's visiting author program—Author! Author!—and cocc.edu for COCC's Visiting Scholar Program.

One example of an event created expressly for the purpose of impacting Bend's culture is TEDxBend. In 2011 a group of Bend citizens who were addicted to the offerings of the worldwide TED Talks videos held the first of what turned out to be an annual springtime event. TEDxBend is a local version of the TED international event and has become, thanks to the Bend High School auditorium that seats 1,400, one of the largest TEDx events in the nation.

Bend's restaurant scene plays a major role in Bend's entertainment culture as well, and was seemingly designed for a community much larger than ours. We were dubbed by *The HuffPost* as "one of the top cities with the most eateries per capita." Kick in a number of unique restaurants in the adjoining communities of Sunriver, Tumalo, and Sisters and you've got yourself a dynamic dining scene. If you can't find the food you're looking for, hang on, there will be a restaurant for it soon!

Writer's Note: Can an In and Out Burger be far away?

Probably the most visible example of Bend's proclivity for art and culture is our roundabout art. A mixture of creativity, craftmanship, and whimsy, our fascinating collection of creative sculptures dispenses enjoyment to Bend drivers as they go about completing their daily business and chores. Thanks to a group of philanthropic Bend citizens known as Art in Public Places, there are, at last count, 24 unique roundabout art exhibits in Bend. For a map of those exhibits, stop by Visit Bend and pick up a Roundabout Art Route brochure.

Bend, as a result of our youthful and energetic demographic, has an active music scene. I have a friend who hails from Dallas and relocated to Bend in 2016. He's a music aficionado and knows his way around Dallas and even Nashville. The only mountain-related experience he'd undertake would be a hike from the Mt. Bachelor parking lot to its bar...and yet...he picked Bend over the rest of the U.S. All for its music scene, he says with a wink.

All of the finest music in the world is no good unless it has the right venue for people to hear it. Enter the Les Schwab Amphitheatre, which draws locals and tourists alike to its variety of world class events. For more on this gem of Bend's entertainment scene, see Appendix C.

Bend's arts and culture scene has grown at least as fast as our population—maybe faster. It won't take a visitor or a new Bend resident long to learn there's so much more to Bend than our mountains and streams. If you're into arts and culture, you're in for a treat.

For a review of some of the key organizations that make up our cultural scene, check out appendix D. You'll also find included in that appendix a listing of our largest festivals and events along with a description of our favorite venues.

CHAPTER 12

A VISION FOR TOMORROW: KEEPING BEND SPECIAL

Back in the mid-2000s, a married couple I know, Randy and Elaine, visited Bend as a stop on their nationwide search for a community where they could settle down. Young (25ish), child-less, and active, they had been traveling the world for three years and were ready for the settling-down stage of life, which for them included family, careers, and fun, most of it of the outdoor variety.

On a warm Sunday in July, Randy and Elaine were wandering around a Bend neighborhood upstream from Mirror Pond. Out of the blue they were greeted by a man mowing his yard.

"New to town?" the man inquired after exchanging greetings.

"We are," Randy replied with a grin. "We're checking Bend out."

"You look fit," the man replied. "Wanna use my kayak? You can check Bend out best from the river."

"Well, uh, sure, that would be awesome," Elaine replied. "But... are you sure? You don't even know us."

"Don't have to," the man shrugged. "This is Bend. Besides, I've got a bum knee and my kayak needs exercise. There's a concert at the Amphitheatre tonight; you could enjoy it from the river. Just drop the kayak off when you're finished."

Thanking the man profusely, Randy and Elaine borrowed the kayak, took in the concert, and determined that same evening that Bend would be their new home. It wasn't the mountains or the river or the idyllic summer day that drove their decision, it was their conversation with that man. A stranger and his kayak.

Every community has a yin and a yang. For Bend, the yin is the "pro-growthers" and the yang is the "slow-growthers" and/ or "no-growthers"; it's our small-town version of our nation's immigration issue. Both factions agree on one topic, however: Bend must not lose its small-town culture as our population grows. The man with the kayak would probably agree.

It's a tangible concern. In 2030 the drumbeat of change will have done its work; Bend will be somewhere around 150,000 strong, with a faster pace and longer lines at our roundabouts. Costco will be selling gas, we'll have a fourth high school and will be planning our fifth, and (hopefully) several In-N-Out Burger stores will dot our town.

All this will happen because Bend's growth is inevitable. What is not inevitable, however, is that our culture must change in lockstep with our population increase. For many of us, Bend still has roughly the same culture that it had when we came to town. Bend was special then and it is still special today.

When you get right down to it, what makes Bend so special is that we're a community of people who forget our differences and get sh*t done. Bend's citizens, especially in today's polarized environment, have come to the understanding that if we can't make things happen in our nation (or state) any longer, we sure as heck can in our own hometown. And so we work even harder here at home.

Not too long ago I ran into Scott Douglas, a friend who is actively involved in Bend's nonprofit scene through his association with the Cascade Relays Foundation. He also grew up in Bend, and other than a stint with the Merchant Marine, he's spent his entire life here.

"Hey, Jim," Scott said. "Rumor has it you're writing a book about Bend."

"In the process," I replied.

"I have a definition you might want to use," he said, "in the event you use the word 'local' to describe us old-timers."

"I'm all ears," I replied.

"A 'local' is not about how many years you've lived in Bend," he said softly. "It's about how much you've given back."

If that's still the definition of a "local" in 2030, Bend will be looking good. It's our job to make sure that that definition still applies.

BEND'S LEADERS:
THE PEOPLE WHO GOT US HERE

Sure, our mountains and streams are inviting and delightful, but other communities have inviting and delightful mountains and streams too. Our region's beauty and utility aside, it's really our past and current citizens who have made and are making Bend the unique community it is today.

Those past citizens are part of Bend's history, and history doesn't just happen; it is the sum of the work of any city's, state's, or nation's people over a period of time. You can't talk about the history of the United States, for instance, without the names of Washington, Jefferson, and Lincoln popping up.

Here's the formula for any community: you start with energetic people, add a dash of time, and whammo, you get history.

Following is my admittedly subjective list of a few of Bend's citizens who have made major contributions to Bend's modern-day history over the past 30 years. I'm sure I've missed some key contributors, and for that I apologize.

The People Who Laid Bend's Foundation

(The late) Pamela Hulse Andrews: Pamela was the outspoken publisher and editor of *Cascade Business News* and *Cascade Arts & Entertainment*. She always had an opinion on the subject du jour and was never shy about expressing it. Attend a meaningful Bend event and you'd see her there.

Neil Bryant: Neil was Bend's state senator for eight years in the 90s and Bend's finest legislator. A highly respected, moderate, pragmatic Republican, Neil would have made a great governor had he lived on the other side of the mountains, where the majority of Oregon's population resides. He is the recently retired "Bryant" in Bend's oldest law firm, Bryant, Lovlien & Jarvis, P.C.

(The late) Bob Chandler: Bob put *The Bend Bulletin* newspaper on the map as its editor and publisher from 1953 to 1996. He was also a hard-charging businessman and philanthropist back in print media's easier times.

Jim Crowell: Jim is Bend's unofficial historian and a man of considerable distinction to those of us who know him. A Bend native, he knows our history and the people who got us here better than most. He's also passionate about fundraising; his projects include the renovation of the old Bend High School, which now houses the Boys & Girls Club. To know Jim Crowell is to understand the culture that makes Bend special.

Gary Fish: Gary built Bend's iconic Deschutes Brewery from the ground up. Deschutes' employees love their company and, in turn, Bendites love Deschutes Brewery. Gary has turned Deschutes into one of Bend's most active corporate citizens.

(The late) Sister Catherine Hellman: Sister Catherine served as president of St. Charles from 1969 until 1995. Over the course of her 25-year reign, St. Charles grew from $1M in revenues to $40M. Today St. Charles is a regional hospital, with hospitals in Bend, Redmond, Madras, and Prineville.

(The late) Bill Healy: In 1958, a $100,000 investment (thanks to 180 Bend donors) bought two rope tows and a Poma lift for the startup of Mt. Bachelor thanks to Bill, its visionary founder. A veteran of the U.S. Army's 10th Mountain Division, Bill brought his love for skiing to Bend and to the hundreds of thousands of visitors that would visit Mt. Bachelor over the years, enjoying its dry powder, snow, and sunshine.

Mike Hollern: Mike is arguably the single largest contributor to the Bend we know today. The board chair of Brooks Resources Corporation, Bend's largest developer, Mike's footprints are all over so much of what is Bend today, from our roundabouts to the Parkway to Awbrey Butte to NorthWest Crossing. A native Minnesotan, he's also one of Bend's most prolific philanthropists.

Becky Johnson: Proving that you don't have to be a Bend old-timer to make a difference, OSU- Cascades' Becky Johnson came to Bend in 2009 and seven years later the university opened its doors. There was a myriad of roadblocks along the way, but Becky persevered, and, thankfully, education won. The arrival of higher education has been the culminating piece of Bend's infrastructure puzzle.

Jim Lussier: Jim was the CEO of St. Charles following the retirement of Sister Catherine and led the hospital through some of its finest years. Everyone knew Jim and Jim knew everyone; he was a hospital CEO of and for the people.

Charley Miller: Charley is a third-generation Bendite, president of Miller Lumber, and active philanthropist. COCC wouldn't be the same without his contributions of time and money. Plus, there'd be no Miller Tree Farm and Miller's Landing Park.

Patti Moss: Patti built Bank of the Cascades (now First Interstate Bank) from a corner bank into a statewide power. She played a key role in bringing OSU-Cascades to Bend and has served on dozens of Bend and State of Oregon boards.

Jim Petersen: Jim is the (retired) "Petersen" in Bend's Karnopp Petersen law firm. He was the board chair of Bank of the Cascades and St. Charles Hospital for many of their finest years and a founder of Volunteers in Medicine.

Rod Ray: Rod is the former CEO of Bend Research (now Capsugel), Bend's first New Economy business. Rod is now into his encore career, the focus of which is to help Bend's leaders grow. A graduate of OSU, he played a major role in OSU-Cascades not only coming to Bend but succeeding once it arrived.

Bill Smith: Been to the Old Mill District lately? Bill is the architect, builder, and visionary behind this popular venue, all wrapped into one. He turned a repository of sawmill rubbish into Bend's second downtown. Bill is a true empire builder; he's changed the face of Bend.

Amy Tykeson: Amy is the former CEO and owner of BendBroadband. The Tykeson family's foundation's major $1 million gift played a key role in OSU-Cascades coming to Bend. Amy is an active board member of many organizations, both in Bend and around the state.

Todd Taylor: Todd Taylor, a fourth-generation Bendite, is the CEO of Taylor NW and has been a contributing board member to dozens of Bend nonprofits. Todd's sphere of involvement ranges from Mirror Pond to OSU to St. Charles, and he and his family are among Bend's foremost philanthropists.

Connie Worrell-Druliner: Connie is the owner and founder of Bend's Express Employment Professionals. She's been on too many local boards to count and knows everyone who has been involved with anything that matters to Bend.

EVENTS, FORUMS, AND CONFERENCES YOU DON'T WANT TO MISS

If someone with plenty of time on their hands ever decides to make a list of all the events that take place in Bend every year, that number would be in the thousands. Of course, those thousands of events would be influenced by the rash of 5K races and pancake breakfasts that fill the summer months, but you get the point. We Bendites love our events.

Not every event is created equal, however. There are events and then there are EVENTS. Following are my Top 12 Bend EVENTS, listed in no particular order. Why 12? Because I simply couldn't leave even one off the following list—and I had to stop somewhere.

Note: These do not include the summertime concerts that rock the Les Schwab Amphitheater on starlit nights, where you're just as liable to hear Willie Nelson as you are the Dave Matthews Band.

Anyway, here we go. My top Bend events:

1. **July 4 Pet Parade and Old Fashioned Festival:** Bend's Pet Parade, which dates back to the 1930s, is a throwback to yesteryear, a glimpse into our nation's past. If Norman Rockwell were still alive, he'd paint it. You can't go to the Pet Parade without feeling a rush of patriotism. While the

Pet Parade is billed as a birthday party for the U.S., it really comes off as a tribute to rural America. Plus, you gotta
love those animals trotting alongside their families—the
dogs, the cats, the llamas. The parade is more about the
people attached to those pets; the moms, dads, and kids
waving their flags, tossing their candy, and hoping their
dog doesn't poop in the middle of the street. Yes, the Pet
Parade is good ol' U.S. of A, Bend style. Thank you, Bend
Parks & Rec, for organizing this outstanding event.
See *bendparksandrec.org*.

2. **TEDxBend:** Usually held in the early spring, TEDxBend
    is the day to shake the cobwebs out of our heads and
    think about how good the world could be if we did what
    the speakers told us to do. TED bills its local TEDx events
    as "Ideas Worth Sharing," but that tagline ought to read
    "Ideas Worth Doing." After all, what good is an idea if noth-
    ing comes of it? In the course of a TEDxBend day you'll
    hear a dozen or so very smart people present a dozen or so
    very cool ideas. *tedxbend.com*.

3. **Cascade Cycling Classic:** The Cascade Cycling Classic is
    North America's oldest professionally staged cycling race.
    The race is a weeklong extravaganza of professional bi-
    cycle racing throughout the Cascades and the streets of
    Bend. For the more adventurous spectator, the first three
    stages can be viewed from the mountains themselves. No
    matter where you decide to view the event, don't miss the
    fourth stage: Saturday night's downtown criterium. Note:
    The Classic is taking a hiatus in 2018 but will be back in
    2019. *cascade-classic.org*.

4. **Bend Venture Conference (BVC):** If you're into entrepre-
    neurship and innovation, here's an opportunity to join 600
    or so other business folks who are too. Billing itself as "the

largest angel conference in the Pacific Northwest," BVC results in a half-dozen or more entrepreneurs walking away with hundreds of thousands of dollars in investments to grow their businesses. The event kicks off on a Thursday night and lasts through Saturday, and the buzz of energy is as palpable as it is draining to those who attend the event from beginning to end. The networking is world-class too, if you're into such chatter. *bendvc.edcoinfo.com.*

5. **City Club of Central Oregon (Monthly Event):** If you're looking for the inside scoop on what's going on in Bend and/or Central Oregon, the nonpartisan City Club is the place to go. You're liable to hear from our school superintendent, the city manager, or one of the county commissioners at this monthly forum. The City Club's role is to educate and promote community conversation. If you want to rub elbows with people who care, add a City Club meeting to your calendar. *cityclubco.org.*

6. **Pole Pedal Paddle (PPP):** This event could only be held in Bend; it is a one-day eruption of downhill skiing/snowboarding, cross-country skiing, cycling, paddling, and straight-out running. PPP is about Bend emerging from another long winter and celebrating the arrival of spring. You can participate in the event by yourself or you can be part of a team. You can do it if you're 60 and you can do it if you're 10. And, lest I forget, PPP is also about good food and even better beer. *pppbend.com.*

7. **Mt. Bachelor Pond Skim:** This nutty, hilarious, end-of-May event marks the closing of Mt. Bachelor and the end of another ski season. Exactly 100 skiers wearing outfits no sane person would ever be seen in come crashing down the mountain on skis (one at a time, fortunately), hopefully gaining enough velocity to propel themselves across a 100-

foot ice-water pond at the bottom of the hill and onto the other side. Most don't make it, to the unbridled enjoyment of the howling multitudes. Check out this crazy event on YouTube if you want a preview. Who are those weird people, anyway? *mtbachelor.com*.

8. **BendFilm Festival:** BendFilm Festival is a beloved Bend event and ranks among the top film festivals in the world. In the middle of October talented independent filmmakers gather to show off their work to audiences craving something more than million-dollar movie stars blowing something up. Over 60 short films round out a robust feature film and documentary lineup, plus you'll have the opportunity to chat with the filmmakers themselves over the course of the event. As many as 14 filmmakers will receive cash awards for their efforts. You won't be lonely if you go, in 2017 8,000 people attended the festival. *bendfilm.org*.

9. **Pub Talks (Monthly Event):** I know, I know, yet another business event, but this one is monthly, or sorta monthly, anyway (nine times a year). Hosted by EDCO, Pub Talks takes place at McMenamins Pub and includes yet another excuse to see good friends and drink great beer. Pub Talks features a guest speaker and two or three feisty entrepreneurs pitching their wares along with up to 300 people throwing their energy around. Watch out, you can get so amped up by what goes on at Pub Talks that you won't be able to sleep at night. *edcoinfo.com*.

10. **Oktoberfest:** Oktoberfest marks the beginning of what the tourist folks call Bend's shoulder season—that span of time between the end of summer and the beginning of ski season. What else to do but host an event that revolves around—you guessed it—drinking beer. Whatever you do, don't miss the wiener dog races, if, that is, you can wiggle

your way in close enough to see the action. Be aware, however, that wiener dog racing can be dangerous. You could die laughing. *bendoktoberfest.com*.

11. **Bend Brewfest:** Here's the beer folks, at it again, edging their way into our pocketbooks and our hearts. Bend Brewfest is an annual August event that gives both locals and visitors a chance to taste some of Bend's and Oregon's finest craft beers. Over 150 craft beers, plus kombuchas, ciders and wines, are on tap and a portion of the proceeds are donated to local charities, including the Deschutes River Conservancy and NeighborImpact. *bendbrewfest.com*.

12. **Munch & Music:** Munch & Music is a series of weekly free concerts over the summertime featuring music, food, and the chance to pull up a lawn chair and watch the small-town world go by. Munch & Music has been around forever, is highly visible and family oriented, and is held in beautiful Drake Park. In addition to the food and entertainment, Munch & Music offers outstanding people-watching; you'll see all sorts of Bend's citizenry at its foot-stomping weekly hoedowns. *munchandmusic.com*

COMMUNITY ASSETS YOU NEED TO KNOW ABOUT

While it's true that Bend attracts people who love the outdoors, many of those people don't come here with the intention of meeting other people just like them. Rather, they come here because we have oh-so many playgrounds in which to float, ride, or ski, and they want to take advantage of every last one of them. For those folks, it's the playground that comes first.

Here are just a few of the cool playgrounds we have in which to play and meet people like us:

Bend's Playgrounds

Mt. Bachelor: Mt. Bachelor stands silent and tall as it keeps watch over us; it is Bend's snow-white beacon in the West. Mt. Bachelor makes Bend's year complete; instead of having seven months to play hard we have 12. Our mountain also attracts tourists, and tourists mean jobs, and jobs mean a healthy economy. Thank you, Mt. Bachelor.

Deschutes River: You can float it, swim it, paddle it, fish it, or hike it. You can do just about everything with it except leave your trash in it. Pull up a log, listen to the Deschutes, and let it be your muse. It is so much more than a river.

Mirror Pond: The Deschutes River takes a well-deserved break at Mirror Pond and so do many of our pensive citizens on its banks. Chock-full of Bend history, Mirror Pond (and its Drake Park partner) hosts everything from car shows to duck races to pancake breakfasts to rock concerts. It's hard to imagine Bend without Mirror Pond.

The Parks: There are 81 glorious parks in Bend, and that number is growing. The king (and queen) of them all is Pine Nursery Park. Don't leave Bend without visiting it. Oh yes, you'll need to watch out for those pickleball players when you're there; it is one of the fastest growing sports in America.

Dog Off-Leash Parks: Because we Bendites love our dogs, Bend Park & Rec builds parks just for them. Well, primarily just for them, but also for their dog-crazy owners who are having just as much fun meeting other interesting people who are dog-crazy too.

Our Back Roads: Thanks to Deschutes County for maintaining our winding, scenic, back-country roads that road-biking enthusiasts use and love. Every day, day after day, rain or shine, in the summer or winter, our back roads are filled with cyclists. Don't they know when to come in out of the rain?

Smith Rock State Park: It may not be located in Bend, but for some it's THE reason they live here. Often called "the birthplace of modern American sport climbing," it overlooks the postcard-perfect Crooked River. There's no better place in Central Oregon for a picnic, all the while watching very buff but unhinged people climbing rocks that are called names like "Monkey Face."

Golf Courses: For those of us who are looking for a sport where we won't get hurt, there are 25 golf courses within a 30-mile radius of Bend. Some are good, some are great, and a few are downright awesome.

Les Schwab Amphitheater: Bend's concert year begins on Memorial Day and lasts until the frost is on the pumpkin. You can enjoy the music while on your feet, sitting on a blanket, or bobbing in a canoe on the neighboring Deschutes River. However you enjoy the music, the stars will be blinking above you.

The Pavilion: Bend Park & Rec thought we didn't have enough to do so they built us an ice rink on which to play hockey, figure skate, or curl. What's next? I wonder. A ski jump? A bobsled track? A velodrome? Stay tuned.

Bend Whitewater Park: The Whitewater Park is a slice of man-made rapids on the Deschutes and near the Old Mill. The waves are angry, and you can surf on them and do tricks. It's also a hangout, a place to learn by watching the experts over your lunch hour. Thirty degrees and snowing? Slither into a wet suit and take a ride. Bend's Whitewater Park knows no season.

Bike Sharing: In Bend, you don't have to own a bike to ride one. Thanks to OSU-Cascades for bringing Zagster's rent-a-bike to Bend.

Food Carts: Are Bend's food carts better than our restaurants? Well, it depends on who you talk to, but they're ubiquitous, and you can wear shorts and a T-shirt while enjoying dinner or happy hour.

ARTS AND CULTURE: ORGANIZATIONS, EVENTS & FESTIVALS, AND PUBLIC VENUES

Examples of Bend's dedication to arts and culture come wrapped in three different packages: 1) organizations that cater to our arts and culture needs, 2) events and festivals those organizations host, and 3) venues for every occasion. Following are examples of all three, with apologies to those organizations, events, and/or venues who, because there are so many, may have been left out.

Organizations: A sampling

Arts and Culture Alliance: See chapter 11.

Cascade Arts & Entertainment: See chapter 11.

Bend Magazine, The Source Weekly and The Bend Bulletin: See chapter 11.

ScaleHouse: See chapter 11.

High Desert Museum: See chapter 11.

Deschutes County Historical Society: In their words, the Deschutes County Historical Society "gathers, preserves and makes available museum, library and other historical material relating to the history of Central Oregon." The Historical Society, and their rustic museum, can be found in the quaint, carefully preserved Reid School, originally constructed in 1914 and now on the National Register of Historic Sites. Bring on old Bend memories. *deschuteshistory.org*.

Bend Art Center: In addition to its art gallery located in Bend's historic Box Factory, the Bend Art Center includes classes and workshops for adults and kids, a center for printmaking and book arts, art talks, and studio rental opportunities. Most of all, the Bend Art Center provides a hub for Bend's artists and the creative denizens of our art community. Previously known as Atelier 6000 (aka A6), the Bend Art Center has a rich 30-year history. *bendartcenter.org*.

Art Station: Formerly Arts Central, the Art Station is today one of many services offered by—here we go again—Bend Park & Rec and provides a wide variety of art classes for youth, adults, and families. The Art Station also offers open-studio options as well as opportunities for parties and groups. See *bendparksandrec.org*.

Bend Theatre Scene: The Bend Theatre Scene provides a central place to find plays along with a current calendar of what's going on in the theatre scene. Check out *bendtheatrescene.com*.

Events and Festivals

See chapter 11 for a listing of the trifecta of publishers who help us keep tabs on what's going on in the arts and culture scene. In the meantime, here is a partial list of the annual events and festivals that Bend's arts and culture enthusiasts have to choose from...

TEDxBend: See chapter 11.

Bend Summer Festival: Drawing upwards of 75,000 people, this annual July event shuts down Bend's downtown and hosts two days of artists, craftspeople, artisans, and performers. (All free, mind you). Boasting three stages featuring some of the Pacific Northwest's best blues, rock, and jazz performers, there's no shortage of things to watch, eat, or drink. Check it out at *bendsummerfestival.com*.

First Friday Art Walk: The Art Walk is held on the first Friday of every month (yes, winter months too). The Walk includes a leisurely tour of Bend's downtown shops, with some of them offering snacks and wine for shoppers. Organized by Downtown Bend, you can check it out at *downtownbend.org*.

Bend Design Conference: The Bend Design Conference is a two-day, multi-partner, collaborative event for "innovators, creative thinkers, and disrupters." Started in 2016, the conference includes two days of conversations, workshops, and exhibits intended to spread the notion that design is more than just an art form, it is also an extension of life. See *benddesign.org*.

Bend Muse Conference: Bend has an incredibly active women's community. Thanks to one woman—Amanda Stuermer—the Bend Muse Conference exists. The Muse Conference brings together local women and teens who, along with internationally recognized women leaders, celebrate International Women's Day at the same time they kick off Women's History Month. Visit *oldmilldistrict.com*.

Art in the High Desert: Held on a weekend in August, Art in the High Desert is Bend's premier juried art and fine craft festival and includes over 100 artists from around the country. Ranked

No. 10 in the nation for fine art fairs, you can find information on this annual event at *artinthehighdesert.com*.

Opera, Jazz, or Chamber Music: There is little that falls through the cracks in Bend's music scene; there's something for everyone. For opera, there's operabend.org; for jazz, try *oxfordhotelbend.com*; and for chamber music, go to *highdesertchambermusic.com*.

Bend Ale Trail: Beer may not be everyone's idea of "culture," but it's definitely part of the cultural fabric for many Bendites. The Bend Ale Trail is a community staple, featuring mostly beer breweries but also a few distilleries and wineries. Organized tourist groups come to Bend for the sole purpose of visiting our brewpubs and tasting our beer. More on the Bend Ale Trail at *visitbend.com*.

Public Venues

Tower Theatre: Boasting a birthdate of 1940 (and later remodeled), Bend's iconic Tower Theatre is the centerpiece for Bend's indoor events, the majority of which are in the performing arts. Billed as "Bend's Living Room," the Tower is also recognized as the culture hub of our community. *towertheatre.org*.

Les Schwab Amphitheatre: See "Bend's Playgrounds."

RULES OF CITIZENSHIP

We are Americans, which, among many other privileges, grants us the inalienable right to reside wherever we choose. This means that Bend's population is going to continue to grow, and there isn't much anyone can do about it. Sure, we can slow growth down—a little, perhaps—and hopefully we can manage it, but in the end, most of us have chosen to relocate here, so how can we, in good conscience, deny that privilege to someone else? We made it here, and so can they.

Once you become a citizen of Bend, however, a caveat kicks in: You are now a de facto protector of our culture, which means that you're obligated to help us preserve what was here when you came. Adopting our culture means being *friendly* to neighbors and strangers alike, being *caring* of our community and those who make it up, and being *respectful* of the environmental assets that brought you here.

Thanks to the good folks at Visit Bend—who have their own version of what being a Bend citizen entails—for inspiring this version of Bend's citizenship rules. I've borrowed several of their gems and added a few of my own.

So, for those of you who have recently won the lifestyle lottery, here's what you sign up for when you become a Bend resident...

1. Make your own memories but not your own trails. Keep our woods and forests the way they came.

2. Cyclists and runners have rights too, and a lot less protection. Nowhere is it written that our streets and roads are for cars only.

3. Use your turn signal always and your horn rarely. Tooting your car's horn enhances no one's Bend experience, including your own.

4. Less social media and more social interaction. Keep your head up when you're walking, not down. (That way you can say hi to the people you pass.)

5. Don't try to circumvent our downtown parking rules. You'll lose. And learn an expensive lesson.

6. We like who we are. We don't need to be like Boulder or Austin; we need to manage our growth and not let it manage us.

7. Tip 20 percent. And other facsimiles of paying it forward.

8. Don't ski alone. Or mountain bike. Or rock climb. Or hike the South Sister.

9. It's OK to disagree but not to rant. Make your point. Then move on.

10. Get involved. Someone else got Bend this far, now it's your turn to contribute.